HYDROPONICS GARDENING

The Complete Guide for Beginners to Build your Own Hydroponics Gardening System

Hydroponic School

© Copyright 2021 by Hydroponic School - All rights reserved. The following Book is reproduced below with the goal of providing information that is as accurate and reliable as possible. Regardless, purchasing this Book can be seen as consent to the fact that both the publisher and the author of this book are in no way experts on the topics discussed within and that any recommendations or suggestions that are made herein are for entertainment purposes only. Professionals should be consulted as needed prior to undertaking any of the action endorsed herein.

This declaration is deemed fair and valid by both the American Bar Association and the Committee of Publishers Association and is legally binding throughout the United States.

Furthermore, the transmission, duplication, or reproduction of any of the following work including specific information will be considered an illegal act irrespective of if it is done electronically or in print. This extends to creating a secondary or tertiary copy of the work or a recorded copy and is only allowed with the express written consent from the Publisher. All additional right reserved.

The information in the following pages is broadly considered a truthful and accurate account of facts and as such, any inattention, use, or misuse of the information in question by the reader will render any resulting actions solely under their purview. There are no scenarios in which the publisher or the original author of this work can be in any fashion deemed liable for any hardship or damages that may befall them after undertaking information described herein.

Additionally, the information in the following pages is intended only for informational purposes and should thus be thought of as universal. As befitting its nature, it is presented without assurance regarding its prolonged validity or interim quality. Trademarks that are mentioned are done without written consent and can in no way be considered an endorsement from the trademark holder.

Table of Contents

INTRODUCTION 6

CHAPTER 1 9

HOW TO BUILD YOUR OWN HYDROPONIC SYSTEM 9

CHAPTER 2 17

BEST PLANTS FOR HYDROPONIC GARDENING AND NUTRITION 17

CHAPTER 3 CHOOSING PLANTS 24

CHAPTER 4 31

GROWING MEDIUM, NUTRIENTS, LIGHTNING IN HYDROPONICS 31

CHAPTER 5 44

HYDROPONICS VS SOIL GARDENING 44

CHAPTER 6 48

MAINTENANCE OF YOUR HYDROPONIC GARDEN 48

CHAPTER 7 55

SYSTEM MAINTENANCE 55

CHAPTER 8 62

POTENTIAL PROBLEM AND HOW TO OVERCOME THEM 62

CHAPTER 9 71

TIPS AND TRICKS TO GROW HEALTHY HERBS AND VEGETABLES ... 71

CHAPTER 10 77

STARTING HYDROPONIC BUSINESS 77

CHAPTER 11	84
BASIC COMPONENTS OF THE SYSTEM	84
CHAPTER 12 TOOLS YOU WILL NEED	88
CHAPTER 13	98
HYDROPONIC SYSTEMS EQUIPMENT	98
CHAPTER 14	104
CHOOSING THE BEST LIGHTING MEDIUM FOR YOUR HYDROPONIC PLANTS	104
CHAPTER 15	114
THE WORLD OF HYDROPONICS	114

Introduction

Hydroponics is used as a controlled agriculture system for growing out of season crops, for producing crops in areas that are less suited for growing crops, and in areas where the water supply cannot support conventional farming. Research centers also take up hydroponics to grow crops they need to study plant nutrition, plant breeding, and plant diseases because the conditions under which the crops are grown can be regulated as desired. Almost all plants can be grown using hydroponics. When crops are grown in this way, they use up 50% less land and 90% less water when contrasted with traditional crop growing methods. However, the yields from the crops are 4 times more, and the crop growth rate is twice as fast when using hydroponics. This is possible because the crops have everything they would need, at the right concentrations.

In place of the soil used in typical agriculture, the farmer or gardener roots the plants in compounds like vermiculite, clay pellets or rock wool. All substances used must be inert so that they do not introduce any new elements into the plant's environment. The solution of water and nutrients is then poured over the support material so that the plant can feed into it.

One primary advantage that hydroponics offer over traditional crop husbandry methods is that when the systems are carefully manipulated and the growing environment properly managed, in terms of the quantity of water provided, pH levels and the combination and concentration of the nutrients. When these conditions are looked into carefully, the crops grow faster. There is less waste in regards to the consumption of resources. There is also less reliance on fertilizers, pesticides and other potentially harmful products used in conventional agriculture.

The development of hydroponics has not only been a response to the current food and resource problems. It is a solution for the future too. Experts say that by 2050, about 80% of all the food produced will be consumed in the cities, which makes it important for the cities to become producers of food. Currently, most cities are the good 'black holes' because all they do is suck in much of it, and at the same time, the cities are the biggest food wasters.

It is easy to see the wastefulness and excessive nature of normal food production in comparison to hydroponics. To supply food to the urban areas, producers need to produce it in large amounts and to transport it there, sometimes, across vast distances, before it is introduced into the market. From the initial step of production, harvesting, packaging, and shipping, the food takes up large amounts of resources that could be saved and re-used elsewhere. People are involved, pollution-causing fuels, buildings, and other resources, and this is wasteful, in comparison to what hydroponics entails. As the world's population is getting close to 7.5 billion and the demand for more food increasing just as fast, with emphasis on resource-intensive foods, it is clear that farming needs to be done even in the cities, and even so, more productively.

Chapter 1

How to Build Your Own Hydroponic System

While there are many sites and businesses out there that will sell you hydroponic kits, it can be very easy to make them ourselves. This isn't to say there is no value in store-bought kits. But before we go spending a lot of money, a DIY setup can be a great way to get a handle on the basics of setting up a hydroponic garden. Once we know what we are doing, we can then start to add on all sorts of gears and gizmos to personalize and level up our gardens. But we have to start somewhere and DIY is a great place to kick off from.

Drip System

For this system, we're going to look at one of the easy-to-build drip systems. This one uses buckets in which to grow the plants which still receive their nutrient-rich water through a series of tubes. In order to accomplish this design, there are three key areas which we need to build: the buckets, the reservoir and the tubing. We will look at what it takes to make a single plant setup but we'll see how easy it is to adapt the system to include more.

Start with your bucket. For our purposes, we'll begin with a five-gallon bucket but you can increase or decrease the size as necessary. The first thing we do is flip the bucket upside down so that we can get at the bottom easily. We're looking to get the drain into place so that any water dripped into the system will be recycled back into the reservoir. To do this we will be using a thru-hole fitting.

These little guys are used in all sorts of different fields and you can easily pick one up for a dollar or two at any hardware store.

Place the thru hole on the bottom of the bucket, thread side making contact, and trace around it. This should give you a small little circle on the bottom of your buckets. We want this circle to be closer to the edge than to the middle, as we want our bucket to be able to sit comfortably on an elevated surface. With that in place, cut out the circle you have traced and insert the thru hole into the bucket. Tighten the thru hole in place. Your bucket now has a drain installed. Take a filter of some sort, can be a furnace filter or any kind really, and cut enough out to place over the thru hole inside the bucket. This helps to keep only water draining and not our growing medium.

Now before we move onto the next step, we should paint our buckets. We can double up this task and paint our reservoirs at the same time. Use a black paint on the outside of the bucket in order to block light from entering which would lead to algae growth. With the buckets painted black, they are going to attract a lot of heat which would raise the temperature of our water and could prove to be a real pain in the long run. For this reason, it is suggested that you use a coat or two of white paint over the black paint so as to reflect the light rather than absorb it.

We're going to do a similar design when it comes to our reservoir but the key difference is the hole we cut will be in the top and not in the bottom. Having painted the reservoir black and then white, we will cut a hole in the top of it through which we can feed the cording for our pump and for the hoses. That's all that the reservoir takes.

But in order to make this work from here, we need to connect them using tubing. Connect the tube to the hose and feed it up to the bucket. You can use glue, tape, or whatever method you prefer in order to keep the tube in place to feed your plants. One effective way is to create a loop that sits inside the inside of the bucket, poke a ton of little holes in it and then connect that tube to your main tube. That way water would flow up through the main tube, connect to the inner bucket tube and it would work like a mini sprinkler system. This way makes sure that the water is spread around the bucket and not confined to a single area.

With the feeder tube in place, we then need to attach the draining tube. This is as easy as hooking our tubing up to the thru hole we inserted and running it back down into the reservoir. It is important that we keep our grow bucket elevated above the reservoir so that gravity can do its trick. In order to make sure that we aren't drowning our plants, it's important that we get a digital timer and hook it up so that we aren't pumping water at all times. We'll want to get a timer that allows us to set many different times rather than just one time because we want our system to turn off and on several times a day rather than just once. We need to do this in order to make sure that our plants are getting the right amount of nutrients.

So that is how you set up a single bucket drip system. If you want to expand the system, it is actually very easy. Let's say that you wanted to do four buckets instead of just one. You take those buckets and you give them their thru holes and a paint job all the same. The major difference between running a single bucket setup and a four-bucket setup is the tubing. Rather than running a single tube from our reservoir to our bucket, we are going to instead use T-connectors.

Take the tubing that runs out of the reservoir and connect it into a T-connector. This will give you a tube that looks like a T-corner like we see on the roads. Instead of being a single tube with one ending, you now have two tubes each with their own ending. This would allow us to use a two-bucket setup. However, we choose a four-bucket setup for this example. This means that we have to take each of those tubes and again run them into a T-connector. Now each side gets split into two and we have four ends, one for each of our buckets and we have quadrupled the size of our grow operation.

With all the building in place, we then just have to pack in our buckets. Some rocks at the bottom of each bucket can serve to help weigh them down but it's not absolutely needed. This is more a precaution, though it is one that is recommended. Over the rocks, you pack in your growing medium and then you get your plants in there.

And there you have it, your very own hydroponic drip system.

Wicking System

As we saw above, wicking is actually the easiest of the systems to get started with. It's also one of the easiest systems to build as it requires very little technical skill. All we need to get started is a growing tray, a reservoir and a material for wicking.

Wicking is simply the use of a wickable material going from our reservoir to our grow tray. This can be rope, felt, string; whatever material you can easily get your hands on for the wicking will work.

We will first set up our reservoir, filling it with our nutrient solution of choice, which of course depends on what we are growing. Again, we are going to paint the reservoir black and then cover it in a coat of white paint to prevent it from supporting algae or growing too hot. We are then going to cut or drill very small holes in the cover of the reservoir through which we will thread our wicks.

Our grow trays are going to be filled with a medium that is particularly well-suited to wicking such as perlite or coco coir. But before we fill them up, we first want to cut or drill tiny holes into the bottom of the tray as we did to the cover of the reservoir. These will be roughly the same size because they are how the wick gets the nutrients to the plants.

Ultimately, we have our wicks almost entirely submerged in the water. This doesn't necessarily mean that they are touching the bottom of the reservoir but they are certainly coming close. They are then fed up and nested in the growing tray very close to the plants. We can use more than one wick per plant depending on the plant's particular water and nutrient needs.

As far as set up, that's really it. We place our plants into the grow tray and we watch how they grow. However, there are some tips and tricks that will make a more successful wicking system. We might consider using an air pump to aerate the water so that our plants are able to get more oxygen as this will help them to grow faster. Another thing we will want to consider is keeping the grow tray closer to the reservoir with a wicking system than we would with a drip system. This is because the nutrients aren't pumped to our plants in this system but have to rely on what is called capillary action (aka, wicking). Having our wicks shorter means, they can more easily provide. The distance between our wicks and the grow tray is one way of doing this. Another is making sure that the level of the water in our reservoir is high, as this shortens the distance as well.

Again, this system isn't great for plants that require a lot of water and nutrients because the wicking of nutrients is a slow process. However, herbs and lettuce can grow great crops in a wicking system and this makes for an easy way to introduce the concepts of hydroponics to someone new to the topic. They even make great projects for getting kids into hydroponics and gardening!

Deep Water Culture

Despite the wicking system being considered the easiest of the hydroponic systems to get started gardening with, the deep-water culture is just about as easy when it comes to building. For our purposes of explanation, we will be making a single deep-water culture. This means that we will be designing one as if we were growing a single medium-size plant. This system can be adapted to fit multiple smaller plants, though if we want to go bigger, we will have to change our culture to a larger container first.

Since a deep-water culture uses deep water (it's there in the name, after all), we will be using a five-gallon bucket because of the depth that it gives us. While some people refer to any system of plants floating on the water as a deep-water system, we actually need to have ten plus inches of water for it to be considered deep. We could grow a small plant in a small culture and have it be equivalent in ratios to that of a deep water culture but it still wouldn't be proper to call it such.

The first thing that we are going to do, surprise, is paint our bucket black and then white. Slightly underneath the lid, we are also going to cut a little hole for the tubing of our air pump so that we can oxygenate the water. With these two steps out of the way, we can set our buckets to the side.

Because a deep-water culture works by having the roots of the plant soaking in the water, we need to design a setup so that our plants can bath. To do this, we can go out and buy what is called a plant basket. This is a basket that looks like your typical plant pot but instead, it has a ton of holes through the lower half. Alternatively, we can also just take a plant pot and then cut, drill or solder holes into it. This is going to be our grow tray.

We'll be filling our grow tray up with our desired growing medium and the plant that we want to raise but first, we need to integrate it into the system. To do this we will be cutting a hole in the lid of our five-gallon bucket. At this point, it is best to cut a smaller hole and make it larger as needed rather than start with a large hole. This is because it is far easier to increase the size of the hole than it is to block it back up. If we make our hole too big, our grow tray will just fall into the bucket and we will need to get another lid and try all over again. Our goal is for the lower half of the pot to fit into the hole and be held in place by the pot's rim against the bucket's lid.

Earlier, we cut a hole in our bucket just under the lid for our air pump. The reason we didn't cut it on the lid itself is that when we open our system up to check the pH levels and make sure our nutrients are all balanced, we don't want to have to fiddle around with any wires. When we open our system, we should only have to remove the lid and thus the plant pot.
Everything should now be in place. We're going to fill up the bucket with our water, bringing it up to cover three-quarters of the plant pot that is hanging down inside it. We might want to test this first with plain water so that we can then mark the desired water level on our buckets to make it easier to see going forward. Mix together your nutrient solution, fill the plant potter with your desired growing medium and add your plant or seed.

It will take a week or so for the roots of the plant to start poking out of the holes that we drilled into our pot, so it is important to make sure that the water level is high enough for our plants to get the moisture they need. As the roots begin to hang down, the water level won't matter nearly as much.
And there you have it, you just created a deep-water culture for your plants. While you can grow a medium-sized plant or a couple of small ones in this one culture, you are most likely going to want to set up a couple. But as you've seen, that shouldn't take very much time at all.

Chapter 2

Best Plants for Hydroponic Gardening And Nutrition

If you are thinking of adapting hydroponics in your household to expand your food list, or to reduce the cost of your grocery expenses, then it makes sense that you also take into consideration of what you can actually grow in the absence of actual soil. When you consider that plants do not require much to grow, you begin to realize that you can virtually grow anything through hydroponics.

Many popular fruits, vegetables, and herbs can be grown in your (or someone else's) hydroponic gardening system. The choices listed below are just the tip of the iceberg. Just about anything that will grow in your local area in the soil can be grown hydroponically. Some of the more popular and common choices are:

Fruits

Cantaloupe

Sometimes called "Rock-melons," Cantaloupes are a roundish, orange-fleshed type of melon which currently holds the honor of being America's most popular melon.
These melons have been being cultivated by humans for over four thousand years. Like just about all fruits, they are high in Vitamin C. They also contain plenty of Manganese and beta carotene.

Raspberries

There are many different types of Raspberry; they are all members of the Rose family. Raspberries are used in a variety of culinary applications and are often made into jellies, jams and used as a pie filling.

These berries are high in dietary fiber and Vitamin C. They also are a good source of manganese and Vitamin K. Aside from the berry the leaves of this plant are also used to prepare tea.

Many varieties of Raspberry are easy to grow, so easy that they may border on becoming invasive. This is an excellent choice for any hydroponic setup.

Strawberries

The strawberry is technically not a berry. It is what is called an "aggregate accessory fruit," which is a fruit which consists of several of a flower's ovaries combining into a single unit. The "seeds" seen on a strawberry are really individual ovaries with an actual seed inside them.

The Strawberry is one of the most popular fruits in the entire world and has been so for thousands of years. It's reputation as a delicious addition to a variety of desserts stretches back to ancient Rome.

Strawberries provide a decent amount of Manganese and Vitamin C and may provide some protection against heart disease.

Strawberries do very well in most hydroponic gardens and are a popular choice among many gardeners.

Watermelon (Citrullus Lantus)

This common North American melon originated in South Africa and has been being grown consumed by humans since prehistory. By the 1700s, watermelons were a common sight in gardens the word over.

The entire watermelon is edible, rind seeds and all. Most often the rind and seeds are discarded, this is a shame. The seeds can be roasted and enjoyed like sunflower seeds and the rind is sometimes pickled or used in salads.

The average watermelon is high in vitamin C and is over 90% water.

Vegetables

Cucumbers (Cucumis sativus)

This vine growing dietary staple needs no introduction. The cucumber has many uses and is easy to grow using hydroponic techniques. This vegetable is just as popular fresh as it is pickled. The cucumber is a little lacking in the nutrition department when compared to the other vegetables on this list. It does offer a moderate amount of Vitamin K and is comprised of over 95% water.

Lettuce

Lettuce is an excellent candidate for your hydroponic garden; it grows easily, has many uses and, depending on which variety you are growing can be a fairly nutritious addition to your diet. The humble head of lettuce contains high levels of vitamin A, beta-carotene and almost an entire day's worth of Vitamin K.

Peas (Pisum sativum)

Peas are technically a fruit, like tomatoes.

There are many varieties of peas. The most common and familiar is the green pea. They tend to grow well in a hydroponic manner and are recommended for beginners.

Peas offer a pretty impressive group of nutrients, including high amounts of vitamin C, vitamin K, Vitamins B5 and B6, vitamin A, dietary fiber. In addition to vitamins and fiber peas are full of minerals such as zinc, copper, lutein, and magnesium. They are also high in sugar, making them an excellent source of energy.

Spinach

Spinach, most popular as Popeye's favorite food, was first cultivated in ancient Persia. It became known in Europe sometime during the ninth century and became a popular dietary staple in the 1500s.

In modern times, spinach has always been valued and praised as an incredibly nutritious plant. Its high iron content alone is enough to justify this reputation, but spinach has much more to offer. An excellent source of Calcium, B complex vitamins, Vitamin A, Magnesium, Manganese, Potassium, and Zinc. A single serving of spinach contains nearly four times the daily requirement of vitamin K. All things considered, fresh spinach is a worthwhile addition to anyone's diet as well as being a great plant to grow hydroponically.

Tomatoes

Oddly enough tomatoes had a rough time making their way into the human diet. They were considered by many ancient peoples to be poisonous, some cultures thought eating them would turn one into a werewolf. Eventually, it was figured out that this was not the case, and people began to see how very useful tomatoes can be in the kitchen.

Tomatoes are a popular choice for both traditional and hydroponic gardens and with good reason. They grow easily, offer a high yield and have many culinary applications. Nutritionally speaking they are an excellent source of antioxidants - compounds which are suspected of having disease-fighting properties. They are high in vitamin C and a great source of trace minerals.

Herbs
Basil

Basil is a very common cooking herb with a myriad of uses. It's a member of the mint family. This herb loves growing in warm sunny climates but does just fine indoors as well. It's a well know repellent of insects and other pests and will help keep them out of
your garden, which makes it worth growing for that reason alone.

Dill

Both the seeds and the leaves of this herb are edible and useful in the kitchen. The leaves are often referred to as "dill weed" and are used to enhance the flavor of many dishes, from soups to roasted meats. Dill weed is used in a similar fashion as Parsley.
Dill seed is often crushed and used as a spice. The seeds are similar in taste to caraway seeds and are used in the same way. Dill seeds are most well known for adding their distinctive flavor to dill pickles.
Dill likes as much sunlight as it can get, even partial shade can inhibit its growth. It is also known to attract helpful insects that prey on more invasive and destructive pests.

Mint

There are many types of mint that are commonly grown in gardens. Mint is one of the world's most popular flavoring agents and is used nearly everywhere - cooking, candies, desserts, gum, etc..

This hardy perennial herb is commonly found growing near water. They also prefer shade to full on sunlight and enjoy cool, moist spots as a general rule. This doesn't mean your mint won't grow well under different conditions - it will, don't worry about that.

Many gardeners find that mint grows a little too well, left unchecked it will happily take over all of your available garden space. Make sure to keep a watchful eye on any mint you have growing. Just one or two plants are usually enough to provide you with all the mint you could ever use. It is common practice to plant mint as a means to keep pests at bay and to attract beneficial insects.
Mint is best used fresh, harvested right before it is going to used.

Oregano

This purple flowered ubiquitous cooking herb is a relative of Marjoram and is sometimes called "Wild Marjoram."
Oregano favors hot and somewhat dry conditions but does well most anywhere.

The leaves of the Oregano plant are often dried and used as a popular addition to many standard Italian-American dishes. Many types of Middle Eastern cuisine also make heavy use of this herb, using it to flavor beef and mutton in addition to using it as a condiment, in the same way many people use salt and pepper.

Rosemary (Rosmarinus officinalis)
Another member of the mint family, Rosemary is grown by gardeners the world over both as a decoration and for use in cooking. The leaves are commonly dried first and used to add flavor to roasted meats and various types of stuffing. Fresh leaves are sometimes used to make a tea. It is also a primary ingredient in some types of vinegar. The essential oil is popularly used as an ingredient in perfumes.

It is easily waterlogged and unsuitable for hydroponic methods that involve leaving the roots of the plants suspended in water all the time. Like just most all the members of the Mint family, Rosemary is sometimes used as a form of natural pest control.

This brief list is just a small introduction to what it is possible for you to grow. A little digging will reveal a list of plants that are due to do well in your particular climate.

Chapter 3
Choosing Plants

"Gardening involves so many disciplines: math, chemistry, reading, history." — David Chang

Let's get started with some basic chemistry. Elements are what a plant uses for its living processes. Over 90% of a plant is made up of four key elements: Carbon, Hydrogen, Oxygen, and Nitrogen. As these elements make up the majority of a plant, it must be able to extract these elements in order grow efficiently. That said, a plant doesn't have to obtain these elements from a completely pure form. For example, although water ($H2O$) is a compound (made up of more than one element), plants are able to extract the elements it needs as pure elements. As the four elements are crucial to a plants life, it's wise to be aware of some of their qualities.

Carbon:

This makes up over half of a plant's composition and is present in chlorophyll and the sugars that chlorophyll creates.

Hydrogen:

Plays a role in the process that results in roots absorbing nutrients. Hydrogen is extracted from water which also assists in maintaining a rigid structure in plants.

Oxygen:

Responsible for respiration which provides a plant energy to grow by creating sugars and starches.

Nitrogen:

Creates amino acids and chlorophyll that manufactures sugars.

Macro-nutrients

Although plants can extract the elements so far from a range of sources, it is 'Macro Nutrients' that generally make up plant solutions.

These nutrients are what a plant extracts in bulk from the hydroponic medium that you use. These elements are Nitrogen (N), Phosphorus (P), and Potassium (K). You'll often see N-P-K levels on pre-made plant food packaging as an indication of strength. Macronutrients play crucial roles and should be regulated to be present in the correct quantities. Too little Nitrogen results in weaker plants with small leaves, while an excess of Nitrogen poses crop-ripening issues. Phosphorus is responsible for fruit and flower creation, but too little results in poor root systems and weak flower generation. Potassium is the driver in protein synthesis which creates sugars and starch, and too little of it significantly slows plant growth.

Micronutrients

There are also other nutrients that plants extract in much smaller quantities. They are rarely in pre-made plant foods, but still have a range of considerable effects on a plant's living processes.

Calcium (Ca): Cell wall creation. Too little stunts growth.
Sulfur (S): Protein synthesis.

Iron (Fe): Chlorophyll development and sugar creation.
Magnesium (Mg): Chlorophyll and enzyme creation. Too little causes yellowing of leaves.

Boron (B): Combines with calcium for cell wall creation. Too little causes week stems.

Manganese (Mn): Creation of oxygen in photosynthesis. Too little causes yellowing of leaves.

Zinc (Zn): Respiration, chlorophyll, and nitrogen metabolism. A deficiency results in small leaves.

Copper (Cu): Enzyme activation; respiration and photosynthesis. A deficiency results in pale and yellow leaves.

Selecting Your Hydroponic Nutrient

Beginner: pre-made nutrient solutions

N-P-K only makes up a part of the solution, with the rest comprising of filler and other nutrients that fuel the growth process. It's vital to remember that you can't use nutrient solutions that are designed for soil use. At first, it's best to search for a solution that is effective at growing a variety of crops. The correct concentration for the solution is crucial as the plants depend on what is mixed into the water that circulates around the system. That said, you'll easily find pre-made solutions with mixing instructions that correspond to your plants and the conditions that you're growing in. This makes things simple if you don't want the extra work of creating your own solutions. A warning - ensure that the packaging explicitly mentions that the nutrient solution is specifically designed for hydroponic practice.

Another factor to consider is whether the solution comes as a one-part solution that is better suited to a wider range of crops and growing conditions, or a two/three-part solution that is more customizable for specific types of crop and the stage in the growing process they are at. You will generally get better results with a two/three part solution, at the cost of being slightly more challenging to develop.

Advanced: mixing your own nutrient solutions

More advanced hydroponic growers often wish to mix their own solutions to suit the type of plants they're growing. In order to do this you will need to obtain the correct salts and dissolve them according to the following instructions. The following mixes create 1 gallon of nutrient solution, but these can be multiplied to suit your needs. For best results, it's important to try to get hold of high quality raw materials. As for the mixing process, fill a container with water warm enough to dissolve salt, and then proceed to dissolving each salt in the outlined quantities. It's best to add and dissolve each salt one at a time.

Nutrient Solution for Vegetable Crops (1 Gallon):

Calcium Nitrate ($Ca(NO_3)_2$): 6 grams
Potassium Nitrate (KNO_3): 2.09 grams
Sulfate of Potash (K_2SO_4): 0.46 grams
Monopotassium Phosphate (KH_2PO_4): 1.39 grams
Magnesium Sulfate ($MgSO_4$): 2.42 grams
7% Fe Chelated Trace Elements: 0.40 grams

Nutrient Solution for Fruit Crops (1 Gallon):
Calcium Nitrate ($Ca(NO_3)_2$): 8 grams
Potassium Nitrate (KNO_3): 2.80 grams
Sulfate of Potash (K_2SO_4): 1.70 grams
Monopotassium Phosphate (KH_2PO_4): 1.39 grams
Magnesium Sulfate ($MgSO_4$): 2.40 grams
7% Fe Chelated Trace Elements: 0.40 grams

Nutrient Solution for Flowering Crops (1 Gallon):
Calcium Nitrate ($Ca(NO_3)_2$): 4.10 grams
Potassium Nitrate (KNO_3): 0.46 grams
Sulfate of Potash (K_2SO_4): 1.39 grams
Monopotassium Phosphate (KH_2PO_4): 1.39 grams
Magnesium Sulfate ($MgSO_4$): 2.40 grams
7% Fe Chelated Trace Elements: 0.40 grams
n. b. The Chelated Trace Element needs to be made up of:
Iron - 7%
Manganese - 2%

Zinc - 0.40%
Copper - 0.10%
Boron - 1.30%
Molybdenum 0.06%

I wish you the best of luck when making your own nutrient solution for the first time! Remember to wait for the solution to cool down before using it within your system.

Managing Varying Concentration and pH Levels

Over time the nutrient solution that you use will change in terms of concentration and pH level. I recommend that you use a digital Parts Per Million (PPM) meter that measures the concentration of salts in your solution. You can then compare the PPM concentration and continuously re-measure in order to keep the concentration of your solution as consistent as possible. This ensures your plant is able to continue extracting what it requires. The pH level of the solution also impacts a plants ability to absorb nutrients. An optimal pH level for plants is generally between 6.0 and 6.5, and to achieve this consistently you can utilize a readily available and affordable pH test and control kit. Easy to follow instructions will be provided with all kits.

By taking the time and effort to carefully control the concentration and pH levels of your nutrient solutions, you will reap the benefits of having plants that grow more consistently and predictably.

Controlling Water Microbes

Another obstacle with keeping your nutrient solution effective is ensuring that the water remains sterile. Harmful anaerobic microbes can occur in your water which offsets the chemical/biological equilibrium in your nutrient solution - this can cause damage to the root systems of your plants. These microbes are likely to appear when water is warm and still, and will be evident from bad smells and brown roots.

To best prevent bad microbes I recommend maintaining the water's temperature between 68-75 degrees Fahrenheit, along with using a pump to regularly move the water around your system. This promotes oxygen and in turn good bacteria (aerobic microbes) that can fend off the bad anaerobic microbes. In order to monitor and regulate the temperature of the water in your solution, I simply suggest using an inexpensive aquarium thermometer.

Now that we've covered how to develop nutrient solutions to promote optimal plant growth, you will next be learning the importance of lighting for the growth of your plants and how you can create efficient lighting for your hydroponic configuration.

Chapter 4

Growing Medium, Nutrients, Lightning In Hydroponics

One of the benefits of hydroponic systems is that there is no soil. In order to compensate for this, the systems need a strong growing medium that stabilizes and supports the plants while also either holding moisture for the plant or draining it away.

In order to feed the plant, because the roots are not in soil, the water needs to have a nutrient solution to properly nourish the plant's roots. Thus, allowing for strong, healthy, fast-growing plants.

Best Growing Mediums for Each System

There are six different hydroponic distribution systems each with their own growing medium needs, although one or two of them do not use a growing medium. Most of the seedlings will start off in one growing medium.

These are some of the most common growing mediums:

- Coco Coir

This organic medium is made from the husks of coconuts. As such it basically has a nearly neutral pH which makes it reusable should it be necessary.
It also retains a good amount of water while supplying an ample amount of oxygen to the root system.
It comes in various different shapes and sizes such as large cubes or small disks for seedlings.

Although it can be used with some hydroponic systems it is not ideal, as it is prone to clogging up systems such as pumps and drains. It is also quite dirty and can add sludge content to a tank.

They are best suited as a growing medium in the following systems:

- Drip Systems
- Ebb & Flow system

• Diatomite

Diatomite is a light, porous growing medium that is made from microscopic algae. This extremely versatile growing medium does not attract insects.

It affords an oxygen-rich environment for the root systems while retaining just the right amount of moisture.

They are best suited as a growing medium in the following systems:

- Drip Systems
- Ebb & Flow
- Nutrient Film Technique
- Water Culture

• Expanded Clay Pellets

This medium does not keep water soaked up for too long. This makes it excellent for systems that need a fast-absorbing solution that will quickly bring water to the roots then allow it to drain away.

Its pH neutral, insects do not think of it as a great place to lay their eggs, and if thoroughly cleaned and sterilized it can be reused.

It is made from balls of clay or clay pebbles that are round porous balls.

They are best suited as a growing medium in the following systems:

- Drip Systems
- Nutrient Film Technique
- Water Culture

- **Glass**

The growing medium is one that comes from recycled glass containers, bottles, etc. As a natural substance is porous and offers a highly aerated toxin-free growing medium.
It is used in a foam form and can be used in a wide range of hydroponic applications.

They are best suited as a growing medium in the following systems:

- Drip Systems
- Nutrient Film Technique
- Water Culture

- **Gravel**

Gravel is a relatively cheap growing medium and can be used in nearly all of the different hydroponic systems. It is also used in aquaponic systems and is a good media bed base.

It can be added to other growing mediums to add a bit more drainage to the mix, which ensures that there is not a lot of salt build-up for the nutrient solution. As salt can become acidic and therefore toxic it is not a bad idea to include a bit of gravel in the growing media if it can be done.

Gravel is not known to retain or absorb moisture but is an excellent support system for plants, ensuring they do not float out of their pots or beds.

They are best suited as a growing medium in the following systems:

- Drip Systems
- Nutrient Film Technique
- Media Beds (Aquaponics)

• Peat Moss

Peat moss is known to retain water while providing excellent oxygenation to the root system. It is called an "inert organic" growing medium which does well in growing environment that allows for a passive system.

It is very fragile and falls apart easily, so it is not ideal in systems that have a lot of water flow. It is better suited in a wick type environment or with flowers such as orchids.

They are best suited as a growing medium in the following systems:

- Wick system
- Deep water culture

• Perlite

Perlite is a growing medium that is better when mixed with another growing medium such as coco coir or vermiculite. It adds aeration and drainage to another growing medium. It should only make up around a third of the mix.

It can also help to prevent the toxicity of the nutrient solution as it prevents the build-up of nutrients.

There are three different grades of perlite: coarse, medium and fine. It is suited to all systems as it is used in conjunction with other growing mediums to make up a full mix.

- Rockwool

Rockwool is one of the most commonly used growing mediums and is used in nearly all hydroponic systems. It is also known as stone wool as it is made from the heating of silica-based rocks and is spun off into a very thin, wire like material that resembles a ball of more delicate steel wool. This makes a growing medium that is great for oxygenating root systems, retaining just the right water ratio, and as it is pH neutral, insects are not interested in making it their home.
It is very versatile and comes in a few different sizes to accommodate most growing applications. It is really ideal for seedlings as it comes in a small portion and tends to help little plants thrive.

They are best suited as a growing medium in the following systems:

- Drip Systems
- Nutrient Film Technique
- Water Culture

- River Sand

River sand can be used in nearly all applications and is usually mixed with some other medium like gravel, vermiculite, and so on.

It retains just enough water to provide the plants root adequate nutrients and oxygen before allowing the solution to drain away.

The only sand that should ever be used in a hydroponic, aeroponic, or NFT environment is river sand.

They are best suited as a growing medium in the following systems:

- Aquaponics
- Drip Systems
- Nutrient Film Technique
- Water Culture

- Vermiculite

This growing medium is much the same as perlite only it is mica that is heated to create the medium. Like perlite, it is not a growing medium that is used on its own; rather it is used in conjunction with another growing medium to improve aeration and drainage.

Nutrients For the Hydroponic Garden

Hydroponic garden solutions may all deliver their irrigation systems in a different way, but they all have one major thing in common. Their nutrient-rich solution is water-soluble, as it is delivered directly to the roots with water.

This nutrient-rich solution is full of various macro nutrients that have been specifically designed to deliver the maximum amount of nutrition needed for the growing plants.

Most of these nutrients are delivered from a pre-mix that is in the recommended ratio to the water in the reservoir tank. This ratio depends on the size of the tank, the delivery system of the solution, and the plants being grown in a hydroponic garden. The granular feeding program is usually provided with the mix in order to help the gardener get the correct nutrient and pH balance ratios for the growing system.

The electrical conductivity, or EC, of the mix is how the concentration of the mix is measured. The EC of the nutrient mix can be measured with an EC meter once the mix has been dissolved in a tank of water.

Plants need the following macronutrients for optimum growth:

- Calcium
- Iron
- Magnesium
- Nitrogen
- Phosphorus
- Potassium
- Sulfur

They will also have to have controlled levels of the following nutrients:

- Boron
- Copper
- Manganese
- Molybdenum
- Zinc

The pH Balance

Not only do the nutrient levels need to properly balance and controlled but for the plants to be able to efficiently absorb these nutrients, the acidity levels in their water solution have to be just right. This balance is called the pH balance and should be between 5.5 and 6.5.

The pH is the concentration of hydrogen ion levels that can be found in a certain solution like water. It is also found in various nutrient solutions and soil content.

Levels of pH are measured on a scale of 0 - 14. With anything above 7 being acidic and anything below 7 is considered neutral or normal. If the nutrient solution is mixed with the correct solution to water ratio for the Hydroponic system, the pH balance will be normal.

The table below, points out some of the main points of each medium.

Medium	Good Drainage	Water Retention	Oxygen Retention	Good Stability	Can Dry Out
*Rockwool Fiber					
*Melted Basalt	✓	✓	✓	✓	✓
*River Rock	✓	✗	✓	✓	✓
*Pumice	✓	✓	✓	✓	✓
* Clay Pellets					
*Hydrocorn					

*Hydroton	✓	✗	✓	✓	✓
*Sand	✓	✗	✗	✓	✓
*Composted Pine Bark	✓	✓	✓	✓	✓
*Coco Coir / *Coco chips	✓	✓	✓	✓	✓
*Vermiculite	✗	✓	✗	✓	✗
*Perlite	✓	✗	✓	✓	✗

Lighting

The lighting for a hydroponics system is extremely important. Especially for seedlings. If seedlings do not get enough light, they tend to get long and spindly, with weird-shaped leaves. This is because they try to stretch towards the light.
Even larger plants need a lot of light, usually up to fourteen hours a day, and seedlings need up to sixteen hours of sunlight a day. If you are growing just one or two little boxes of seedlings or a large plant or two, it is easy to pop them onto a sunny window ledge for the day. Although even that is not an ideal situation, because the concentration of the light can also affect the plants.

Just like the nutrient solution has to be the perfect ratio of water to nutrient, and then timed perfectly to water the plants, the lighting has to be done in a similar way. It must be timed to give the plants almost the exact amount of imitated sunlight a day and it must be set at the right intensity so as not to burn the plants or give too little that they are cold.

Balance is crucial for hydroponics system in order to make the system function correctly and produce healthy, nutritious plants. In order to get sunlight to the plants in a hydroponic system, one would have to have a grow light, preferably one that is set to a timer. Having to manually start and then stop the timer may save on buying costs of the timer, but it could also lead to a whole lot of problems.

Pros of manually setting the growing light timer:

- Saves on the cost of buying an automatic timer.

- It allows a person to control the times they switch the lights on and off.

- It can be efficient in energy management.

Cons of manually setting the growing light timer:

- Possibility of human error.

- Possibility of losing entire crops due to human error.

- Very time consuming and the gardener's day has to be timed around being able to switch the timers on and off to ensure maximum growing health.

Granted some of the fanciest timers can be quite expensive but to start out, all a person needs is a mechanical timer with the pins. These are more than adequate for setting up the lighting timers for a few days up to two weeks at a time. Some of them can be shared between two devices.

There are also inexpensive digital ones that may not have all the bells and whistles but still do everything that needs to be done. If you are going to have growing lights, you are going to need a timer.

Pros of a growing light timer:

- No human error

- The timer switches the lights on and off at the exact times the plants need the lights on and off.

- Except for checking to see if the timer is working, the gardener's day does not have to revolve around rushing to ensure they switch the lights on and off at a precise time each day.

- Happy plants that have their needed sunlight time, when and how they need it.

Cons of a growing light timer:

- An initial cost outlay.

- Digital or electrical timers are reliant on electricity.

The Advantages of Using Growing Lights:

- Seeds germinate more rapidly in the correct light.

- Winter germination of seedlings is more successful.

- Seedlings grow up healthier, their growth is not stunted, and in some cases, their growth rate is increased.

- Plants need more daylight hours, some up to fourteen hours a day. This is hard to achieve with natural sunlight and in winter it is impossible. Growing lights make having fourteen hours a day of uninterrupted light possible all year round.

- The correct light in the growing room helps to keep the entire environment healthy, especially if the environmental conditions are all balanced. Such as the correct ventilation for optimum airflow. This promotes good air quality and the correct amount of light to provide both a bit of warmth and light.

The Best Color Growing Lights for Plants

To humans, sunlight is that big yellow ball of light in the sky that makes everything bright yellow or white. But daylight in respect to color is a bit more complex than that. The light we see is what is known as visible light, that is seen through frequencies and wavelengths the human eye can interpret.

What are Spectrums?

Light itself is made up of various spectrums of color that can be interpreted at different wavelengths which is the reason light is described in frequencies or wavelengths. For instance, when you look at a rainbow each color comes back to the human eye at different frequencies. Each color is a different spectrum, and most grow lights only need a dual spectrum light. Dual spectrum means two colors, and for optimum growth those two-color spectrums are red and blue.

Full Spectrum Growing Lights

A full spectrum light is not very energy efficient and can get quite hot as it is usually a fluorescent light that is designed to emulate the midday sun. It does have cool and warm tones, but it is better for a larger growing area with the need for stronger lighting. It could be a bit of overkill for a small-scale growing area.

High-Intensity Discharge (HID) Growing Lights

These are the brightest and most used of all the grow lights. They are a light that is powered by a glass tube containing a gas, usually xenon, that can emit up to 800 watts of light. This light is a lot more energy efficient than fluorescent lights and is more than adequate for a healthy indoor garden.

There are two kinds of HID lights:

- High-Press Sodium Growing Lights

  o   This light is good all-round and is especially good for seedlings as it has a red spectrum and the visible light is amber or orange.

- Metal Halides

  o   These are the perfect grow room light as they emit a white or blue light that is closer to natural daylight and fluorescent lights. They are great for speeding up and ensuring a healthy growth rate for plants and seedlings.

T5 Growing Light

The T5 light is another light that is very good for growing healthy plants and seedlings. It is similar to fluorescent lighting but is a lot more efficient. It is a full spectrum light that is perfect for any type of indoor growing situation. This light is the closest light to emulating daylight as you are going to get.

Chapter 5

Hydroponics Vs Soil Gardening

Advantages of Hydroponic Gardening

Farming and gardening methods are changing and improving, much like technology. The soil-less technique or hydroponics is fast becoming popular because it gives farmers and gardeners less to worry about.
Hydroponics allows plants to grow in nutrient solutions instead of soil, which leaves tilling, weeding, fertilizing, pesticide spraying and cultivation out of the picture. Moreover, better results can be achieved in shorter amounts of time. It is an easy and more efficient way to grow vegetables, fruits, and flowers. Also, the produce is healthier and contains more nutritional value.
Hydroponic gardens can be maintained indoors and outdoors and are very undemanding and inexpensive to maintain.
Here are some key advantages of using hydroponic systems:
Hydroponic gardens require no soil, so even if you live in an area where soil quality is poor, your plants will thrive beautifully. Crops can be grown in greenhouses and even in desert regions.

Hydroponic gardens require less land surface. Plants can be grown in mediums that can be placed in high-density areas or multi-story buildings. The hydro units can also be stacked.
Hydroponic gardening ensures a high yield in a controlled environment. The needed nutrient environment can be maintained and provided to ensure plant growth and productivity. Compared to soil cultures, a small space can produce about ten times the size of plant matter.
Hydroponics promotes water conservation. Plants are fed an accurate amount of water for their needs. If you grow plants in soil, you will require 90% more water to nourish the plant compared with a properly designed hydroponics system. Labor for watering is also avoided as the water stays within the hydroponic system.
Hydroponic gardens and farms can be set up in places with cheap water and power. When established in close proximity to places where there is a high demand for a particular crop, transport and shipping costs are reduced.

Hydroponic gardening eliminates the need for pesticide and herbicide. It is possible to go organic with this set-up. Likewise, it is easier to eliminate plant diseases and pests.

Hydroponic gardening ensures that there is no nutrition pollution to the environment. Aeration is made possible and the risk of calcium, potassium, and phosphorus run-off is easily prevented.

Hydroponic gardeners and farmers do not have to mulch, weed, till and change the soil. It is also easy to harvest crops.

Disadvantages of Hydroponic Gardening

There are many benefits to hydroponic gardening. Lack of land, frequent supply of water and other environmental concerns can be conquered with hydroponics. With the right knowledge and proper techniques, it is a valuable system for commercial farmers and gardeners, but while hydroponics poses many benefits to modern gardening and farming, there are also disadvantages that come with it.

For one, the initial cost to set-up a properly designed and effective hydroponic system is high. In the long run, the conservation of water and nutrients may prove to be inexpensive but before you can enjoy those benefits, you need to set-up a hydroponic system with all the necessary equipment. Hydroponic equipment does not come cheaply. Additionally, technical knowledge and skills are required to maintain the equipment.

Other disadvantages of hydroponic garden systems are the following:

Compared to farming in large fields, hydroponic gardening may yield limited production.

Hydroponic gardening requires constant supervision. You need to be responsible and diligent because the plants depend on you for their survival.

If you do not have sufficient knowledge, you will have to go by trial and error. Some plants will flourish while others may fizzle. You should be prepared to encounter frustrations and disappointments.

Hydroponic gardens are interrupted and influenced by power outages and pump failures.

Because there is no soil to act as a buffer, the plant will wither and die rapidly once the system fails. If interruptions occur, the plants must be watered manually.

Should a water-borne organism or disease appear in your set-up, it will quickly spread and all of the plants will be affected. Hence, vegetative growth and production is disturbed.

 As with any project, make sure you consider all aspects and count the costs before you decide to set-up your own hydroponic system

Chapter 6

Maintenance of Your Hydroponic Garden

Hydroponic gardens need to have the proper care and maintenance, or they will not produce healthy plants. Not only do they need to be constantly cleaned, but there are various maintenance checks that need to be carried out in order to make sure the system remains functioning correctly.
A faulty drain, or a leaky pipe or switch could do serious damage to a hydroponic garden as most of the systems rely on their equipment and parts to work smoothly.

Cleanliness

In order to stop the build-up of algae, mold, and fungus or to stop attracting pests, keep the growing room as clean as possible.

Equipment should be flushed and cleaned at least twice a month to maintain water levels, stop algae growth, and ensure that there are no pests lurking about the system.
In order to stop pests and various fungal growth, growers should always make sure their hands are clean. Hands should be kept washed especially after handling anything that was dirty or in contact with a harmful substance.
Do not let old fallen leaves, stems, fruit, produce or growing media or even pots or discarded trays lie around the growing areas. Rather throw out any debris or broken items, and wash and pack away any unused equipment.

Wash all equipment after use and only reuse a growing medium if it can be reused and it has been thoroughly washed and sterilized. In fact, all growing mediums, whether old or new, should be thoroughly washed before being used as not to contaminate the grow pots, grow trays, and the reservoir. Keeping the growing area and equipment clean cuts down on the chances of infestation and development of frustrating diseases that are a nuisance to get rid of.

Nutrient Solution

The proper nutrient solution for the plant type and system type should be used at the correct ratio of solution to water.
Only use good quality nutrient solutions with an organic base. Advance nutrients are only required should there be a problem that needs to be fixed, such as a nutrient deficiency in a plant. The nutrient solution balance should be checked on a regular basis especially is it is a recovery system where the solution is being continuously recycled.

Make sure that the solution is flushed and completely refreshed on a regular basis and that there is no salt buildup, since this is very acidic and toxic to the plants.

Watering

Watering is done in many different ways and is delivered to each of the hydroponic systems differently.
Make sure the water is always fresh and checked on a regular basis. Algae is a common problem, as is nutrient build up in the system. An oxygen pump should be installed in order to ensure the water is being well hydrated and to keep the water fresher for longer.
Water solutions can come from the tap, drain systems, or rain collection tanks.

Watering can be on a continuous flow basis or set by a timer that switches on and off at different intervals during the day.

If possible, a person should always have a backup water solution available in case of an emergency and their primary watering source is unavailable. Some plants are very sensitive to their watering schedule and even a few minute's downtime and a missed watering schedule can cause some damage.

Reservoir Temperature

The water in the reservoir should be around 65 to 75 degrees Fahrenheit, which is basic room temperature. Water that is either too hot or too cold can damage the plant's root systems and their leaves.

The reservoir should be topped off with water in order to keep pH and nutrient levels constant. Change out the water on a regular basis.

Humidity

Different plants and hydroponic systems need the humidity to be on different levels. There are thermometers that can measure the humidity and temperature to ensure that the plants are comfortable. Keeping an optimum level does not encourage the growth of unwanted diseases and fungi.

Make sure plants that love the hotter temperatures get enough humidity by giving them a regular misting spray. This will help to keep the humidity constant for the plants that do not like too much humidity.

Inspect the Equipment

The equipment should be thoroughly inspected on a regular basis.

There are a lot of things that can go wrong in a hydroponic system, especially with the equipment. And the best way to troubleshoot is to try to avoid as many equipment malfunctions as possible.

The best way to inspect equipment it to keep the entire system in mind. When doing the inspection start at one point and work your way through your system.

Start with the reservoir and all the systems that are dependent on it.

Water feeding pipe

This should be thoroughly checked for crimps that may not be feeding the solution correctly.
Nutrients build up in the pipes so they may need a thorough flushing out or replacing.
Check for any blockages in the pipe.
Check for any holes or leaks that could deter the flow of water pressure in the pipe.
Check for any algae or mold that may be growing in or around the pipe.

Determine if it may be time to replace the hoses.
Give them a good cleaning if they are still viable.
Nozzles and hoses
Check the nozzles that feed the root systems, sprinklers, or misting systems.

When last were they changed?
Check for blockages or leakage.
Check any joins and washers for leaks.
Check for sediment build up, algae, or mold growing in or around these attachments.
Give them a good cleaning if they are still usable.
Drain siphons and hoses
Check the drain pipes for blockages
When last were they replaced?
Check for leaks.

Check for algae or mold growing in or around these pipes.
They may need to have a good cleaning as part of the system maintenance.
Check the reservoir water pump
Test the pump
Make sure it is still working correctly and pumping the water at the optimum flow.

Check that all pump attachments are not leaking air.
Check the reservoir
Check that there is no build-up, algae, or mold growing on the reservoir.
Check for any leaks.
Make sure the water is at the optimum temperature for the hydroponic system and plants.
Check that any air pumps are functioning correctly and adequately oxygenating the tank.
Make sure any oxygen stones do not have unwanted algae or mold growth on them
Growing trays
Make sure the growing tray(s) do not have any leaks in them.
Make sure the growing tray(s) are clean and have not unwanted algae or mold growing on them.
Clean off any nutrient build up and make sure the trays are clean.
For a closed system, the trays must be given thorough flushing out.

Growing pots

Check that each of the pots is still intact and not broken.
Replace any that are not functioning correctly.
Make sure any growing medium is clean and does not have any unwanted algae or mold growing on them that could upset the plant's natural balance.
Lighting equipment
Check that the bulbs are still functioning correctly.
Check that the lighting is still adequate for the environment.
Check the timers are working correctly.
Clean any residue off the lighting system.
Temperature
Make sure that any thermostat is working correctly, and that room temperature is normal.
Check that the humidity is correct for the growing environment.
Check both the temperature and humidity thermometers to ensure that they are still working correctly.

Ventilation
Make sure that there is adequate ventilation in the growing room.
Not enough ventilation can cause mold.
Check that all fans and cooling systems are working correctly.
Support Systems
Check that any hanging supports for the plants are working without causing the plant or system any undue stress.
Make sure that the environment in which the hydroponic system is housed offers the correct infrastructure for the system to function correctly.
Make sure the plants are all supported and planted correctly to ensure a successful infrastructure.
Tools
Are all the gardening tools in working order?
Are they cleaned?
Are there any that may need to be replaced?
Look at Your Plants
Make sure you keep a vigilant check on your growing plants. Measure their growth rate, root growth and when they are ready to harvest.
This gives a person a good measure of how the next batch should perform and something by which to determine if the growing medium, solution, or systems structure may need to be changed or optimized.
The plants must also be checked to make sure they are getting enough nutrients, they are growing as they should, and there are no pests or other infestations. A lot of growing problems and deficiencies can be caused by various infestations. Some are easy to spot, others may take more of an experienced eye, but as a gardener gets to know their plants they will come to instinctively know when something is wrong.
Look for the signs in seedlings such as slow growth, looking sad and droopy, white fluffy stuff growing on the leaves, etc. Take the time to look over the plants; do not just rush through it. If there are a lot of plants to look over, break them into groups and do a revolving sweep of one group on this day, and the next group on another.

If there is an outbreak, you will need to go through the entire growing area right away.

Spending time with the plants in a hydroponic environment can also be quite good for the mind and spirit. Plants and running water are rather therapeutic and can reduce stress, anxiety and ease tension.

Change One Thing at a Time

If you are wanting to change or expand your system, do not try and do it all at once.

Choose a portion to change, switch it around, or upgrade and start with that.

Before rushing out and buying expensive parts, why not try a bit of DIY and try to make it yourself. Or at least look around to see what you have available before rushing off to spend more money on an item you do not really need.

Hydroponic systems are not only flexible and versatile in what they can grow or how they deliver their solutions, but they can also be easily adapted to suit the grower's needs and lifestyle. There are so many great DIY ideas on how to create the perfect hydroponic garden online these days that it is well worth a try. The money you save building the system yourself can be better spent on plants, growing media, or nutrient solutions.

In order to keep a system simple and working for you, think carefully about an upgrade or addition. Plot it out and then work through one portion at a time getting that part right before moving on to the next.

Chapter 7

System Maintenance

These are tips and tricks from experienced growers who have experimented a lot over the years and want you to be as successful as they are.

1.	If you are looking to build your hydroponics system from recycled material, don't forget to check out Craigslist. So many people do their best to give away the things they do not need and you may even find an entire hydroponics system for free or for a very low price. You should also check out the local yard sale sites and you will also want to check out local yard sales. Hydroponics systems can literally be made out of anything that you find around your house or at local sales; all you have to do is be a bit creative and look for the system that works for you.

2.	If you do not want to keep your hydroponics system in the house and you do not want to worry about your plants getting enough light, you can set up your hydroponics system in a greenhouse. Greenhouses are very easy to put together and you can purchase small ones for quite cheap if you do not have a lot of space. Having a greenhouse is going to take the hydroponics system out of your house, ensure that your plants are getting the right amount of light, and reduce your issues with humidity. If you do want to use a greenhouse, you need to consider how you will get electricity to your system. It is important for you to think about this in advance so that you do not get your entire system set up in your greenhouse and then realize that you do not have any way to get electricity to your system.

3.	Make sure that you know the equipment you will need for your system and why you will need it. I hope I have done a good job at explaining what you will need for your system and why you will need it, but it is important for you to know this because not knowing your system is one of the reasons many people fail at hydroponics. Many people think that they can take shortcuts with their system, cutting out vital equipment that the system needs and soon, they find out that the system will not work the way they thought it would. This often leads to discouragement and the person will give up on hydroponics, blaming the system for the issues and not realizing that they did not follow the directions. Make sure you follow the directions when it comes to your system and the equipment you will need.

4.	Use a three-part hydroponics nutrient solution. The three-part nutrient solution is going to be the best for your plants, providing the right nutrients in the correct proportions. Your nutrient solution is very important when it comes to the growth and health of your plants. If you do not provide your plants with the best nutrient solution possible, you are going to find that your plants do not do well and your yields are going to be very low.

5.	You should not keep your hydroponics garden outside unless the temperature is above 55° F. The great thing about a hydroponics system is that it can be moved outdoors in the summer months and indoors during the winter months. This means that you are going to be able to have healthy, fresh fruits and vegetables all year round. It is also a great idea to grow the summer foods during the summer months, when the growing season is coming to an end, clean your system, move it into the house and plant the fall foods. This will not only give you a variety of foods, but it will mean that you have less to worry about when it comes maintaining specific temperatures for your system.

6. Check your nutrient reservoir each and every day. If you have a pump in your system, it is important for you to check the pump on a regular basis because if your pump stops working, your entire system can collapse within a few hours but you also need to check the levels of your nutrient solution. If you do find that the levels are low, simply add some extra water to the reservoir. You do not want to add extra nutrient solution because the nutrients can build up on the roots of the plants and cause a toxic environment. Also, if you are continually adding nutrient solution to your reservoir, the nutrients will never deplete and you will never have a really good time to clean your system.

7. When you are cleaning your system, you need to move quickly. It is important to clean the inside of the reservoir to ensure that algae does not grow in it and deplete your nutrient solution, but you do not want to allow your plants to dry you either. Cleaning the system needs to be done at least once every 10 days and it can be something that can cause a bit of dread because of the amount of speed that is needed to clean it but once you get into a routine, it will get much easier. I would advise that before you start, you get all of your supplies together, that way you do not have to run around gathering your supplies while your plants have no nutrient rich solution available to them.

8. Minimize the amount of light that reaches your nutrient rich solution. The light is what will allow the algae to grow. If a lot of light is reaching your solution, you will have a lot of problems with algae, you will have to clean your reservoir more and you will be wasting a ton of your nutrients and doing nothing more than feeding algae.

9. Stay out of your garden after you have been in another garden or if you have been outside. This is especially true if you have your garden indoors. I stated earlier that you will not have to worry about bugs because there is no soil, but if you are in another garden that does have bugs, they can hang on to your clothes and make their way to your garden, completely destroying your plants in no time. Instead, shower and change your clothes before visiting your garden, just to make sure that you do not bring any little hitchhikers home with you to your healthy garden.

10. Never allow your pets in your garden. The reason for this is the same as the last tip, but it is also because some animals will spray or urinate on the plants simply because they smell like outdoors. They will also chew on the plants if they are able to reach them. Another reason is that you do not want your dog drinking the nutrient rich solution and you do not want his saliva in your solution. Finally, if you have a large animal or an animal that likes to climb, you run the chance of having your entire system knocked over and all of your plants, nutrient rich solution and medium spilled onto the floor.

11. Before you add any new plants to your garden that you have not grown yourself, you want to put them in quarantine for at least two weeks. You do not want any pests being brought into your hydroponics system from the greenhouse or nursery, nor do you want any diseases being brought into your system. To avoid this, simply keep the new plants away from your hydroponics system for a minimum of two weeks.

12.   If you are transplanting from soil, it can seem almost impossible, but it is very easy to do. All you need to do is gently dip the roots of the plant in water, allowing the water to wash the soil away. You do not want to rub the roots because you could break them very easily and you do not want to spray them with a hose for the same reason. You do not have to worry if you cannot get every speck of soil off of the roots because as your nutrient rich solution washes over the roots, it will remove the extra bits of soil. This soil will not hurt your system as long as it is not huge clumps and it will settle to the bottom of your reservoir once the solution has rinsed over the roots.

13.   Do not allow visitors into your garden. The reason for this is the same reason that you do not want to visit your garden after being outside.

14.   Do not try and mix your own nutrient rich solution. It is tempting with all of the DIY recipes out there, but it is so much easier and safer for you to simply purchase the nutrient rich solution from your local gardening center. If you are mixing your own nutrient solution, you are not going to be able to guarantee your plants are getting the amount of nutrients they need. However, if you purchase the nutrient rich solution, you will know that your plants are getting what they need and you will know what they are getting.

15.   Be very careful when you are adding your additives as well. You do not want to purchase cheap additives and you do not want to try and make them on your own. No matter what you are adding to your system, you want to make sure that it is regulated to ensure the health of your plants.

Hydroponics are quite easy, even though they may seem very complicated when you break them apart and look at all of the different components. Not only is hydroponics growing much easier than traditional growing, but it is also much more fun. Weeding and fighting bugs is not fun, but growing healthy, vibrant food is.

Chapter 8

Potential Problem and How to Overcome Them

Hydroponics gardening is not without challenges. This chapter will cover the potential problem and how to overcome them.

Crop health

One of the most significant issues with hydroponic crops, or any crop, is the risk of disease or pests. Either of these can quickly destroy your hard work and leave you without a crop. That's why it is so important to know how to deal with these issues.

Disease

There are several ways in which disease can occur or be introduced to your plants. It is essential to be aware of what these are to prevent them from becoming an issue when you are growing your crops.

Root disease

You won't be surprised to learn that root disease affects the roots of your crops. It is generally caused by a lack of oxygen getting to the plant's root, effectively making them rot. In a hydroponics system, your roots may be in the water all the time, increasing the risk of root disease.
However, providing you maintain the levels of dissolved oxygen and keep the water moving, you shouldn't have an issue with root disease.

Wash hands

Consider for a minute the number of different items you touch daily and you will quickly get an idea of the amount of dirt and contamination that you can carry unseen, on your hands. This dirt, or bacteria, can be harmful to your plants, introducing bacteria that they don't know how to defend against. To prevent this from being an issue, you must always wash your hands or sanitize them before you enter your growing space and handle the plants or the system. Shoes and clothes are equally important.

Sanitize grow materials

A three percent bleach solution or a three percent hydrogen peroxide solution is the best way to keep the growing environment clean. Wipe every piece of equipment and surface with the solution after every harvest. This will prevent bacteria from getting to your plants and potentially killing them. Keeping the area clean doesn't need to be difficult or time-consuming; it just needs to be consistent.

No organic material

Hydroponic systems don't use soil, which is good as soil carries hundreds of different bacteria. Many of which can be harmful to your plants.
However, just because you don't use soil doesn't mean that soil contamination can't happen. You will need to consider where your seedlings came from. If they were initially grown in soil, they are going to need to be cleaned thoroughly before being planted in the growing media.
Keeping all soil and plant material away from your hydroponic system will help to protect your plants. It is better to grow from seed instead of buying a seedling from the gardening store.
Possible Pests
Here is a list of possible pests. Afterward, I will give some tips on how to get rid of them organically.

Aphids
These tiny black or sometimes green dots can quickly suck the goodness out of any plant. They walk along the stems and suck the sap from the plant. This removes the nutrients and will make your plant ill; eventually, it will die.

Some of the most said aphids are greenfly and blackfly. They can breed incredibly quickly. It is important to treat them as soon as you find them; you don't want these pests spreading over to the rest of your crops.
An aphid (can be green or black)

Caterpillars

You already know what a caterpillar is. On its way to becoming a beautiful butterfly, it will chew through every green leaf it can find.
A lettuce eating caterpillar

On the plus side, these pests are relatively easy to pick off and remove; check the underside of your leaves where they usually hide.

Squash Bugs

Unsurprisingly, these bugs are most commonly found on squash plants. They may not be an issue to you if you are not growing any squash.
They look very similar to the stink bug, are approximately half an inch long, and have flat backs. The squash bug is gray and brown with orange stripes on the bottom of their abdomen.
A squash bug (picture courtesy of Donna Brunet)
You'll usually find them on the underside of your leaves in a group. They can fly but generally prefer to walk on your plants. These bugs will destroy the flow of nutrients to your plants.
Mealybugs

This is yet another pest that multiplies quickly once they find a home. They tend to prefer warmer environments. Your hydroponics setup will probably be ideal for growth! The amount of damage they do will depend on the number of pests you have; early detection is crucial. Mealybugs are oval insects approximately a quarter-inch long and covered with a white or gray wax.

A mealybug

Cutworms

The cutworm is the larvae of several different species of adult moths. They will generally hibernate for the winter months; unless your hydroponic system is warm enough to discourage this.

A black cutworm

Once they finish hibernating, they will emerge and start eating the leaves of your plants. They generally feed at dusk; this is the best time to see them in action. They are effectively caterpillars but are often considered grubs. The exact size and look will depend on the species.

Hornworms

You are most at risk of getting them if you have tomatoes. They are green, generally fat, and look like caterpillars.
The adult moth lays eggs on the underside of your leaves in the late spring. These will hatch in less than a week. You will then have larvae, which will start to eat your plants for the next four to six weeks until nothing is left but the stems.

A hornworm

They will generally go into a cocoon for the winter, but if your system is warm enough, they may only do this for a couple of weeks. They can then transform into moths and lay more eggs to feed on your plants.

What might surprise you is the size of the hornworm; it can be as much as five inches long! They are pale green and have white and black markings. They also have a horn at their rear, although this looks dangerous, they are not capable of stinging you.

You will find dark green droppings on the top of your leaves; this will tell you the hornworm is present; turn your leaf over to see them.

Dealing with Pests

Having a greenhouse where soil-based plants are located is a bad idea. Pests could use the soil as a breeding ground before they move on to your hydroponics setup.

Growing your produce from seed will drastically eliminate the possible pests that are on a plant. The plants you buy from your local dealer could be filled with pests already.

Sap Suckers

One of the best natural remedies for sapsuckers is to spray your plants with chili or garlic spray. However, these can affect the taste of your crop and in large quantities, can make it uncomfortable for the plants.

Moderation is the key.

Caterpillars

The simplest way of getting rid of caterpillars is to spray a substance called Bacillus thuringiensis. You should be able to get this in your local garden store.

It is a natural soil-borne bacteria that kills caterpillars and their larvae.

Mold & Fungus

Potassium bicarbonate is excellent at destroying virtually all molds and fungus. You can spray it directly onto any affected plants and the ones next to them.

Beneficial Insects

Another great way of dealing with pests in your system is to use beneficial insects. As the name suggests, these are insects that will help your system by eating the pests that do damage. It is a good idea to have them in your system year-round. That means when there will be an outbreak, they might be able to limit it or negate the outbreak.

Although it might not be easy to introduce them to your outdoor system, it is preferably done indoors or in a greenhouse where they are contained.

Some of the best ones to consider are:

Ladybugs

These are great at getting rid of aphids before they can do any real damage. One ladybug can consume as many as five thousand aphids per year!

A ladybug

Parasitic Wasp

This tiny wasp doesn't sting. It will lay its eggs in the body of an aphid. The baby wasp eats the inside of the aphid before emerging to repeat the process.

The Parasitic Wasp

Praying Mantis

These slightly strange looking creatures are excellent at eating aphids, caterpillars, potato beetles, leafhoppers, hornworms, squash bugs, and pretty much any pest that could be a problem for your setup.

A praying mantis

Lacewings

These are good at attacking virtually all types of pests. They can eat as many as one hundred aphids per week. They also work best at night when most of the pests are active.

A lacewing

It is worth noting that if you had a one thousand square foot greenhouse, you would need approximately two thousand lacewings. You can get these from most biological insect vendors, or you can try planting flowers that attract lacewings near your system.

Good flowers to plant are fennel, dill, coriander, dandelion, and angelica. They also like brightly-lit windows.

Spider Mite Predators

The tiny spider mite can suck the nutrients out of two hundred different plants. Fortunately, you can solve the issue by introducing the bright orange spider mite predator. They may only live for roughly forty-five days, but they can consume as many as twenty spider mites each day!

Aphid Predator Midge

These tiny little bugs look like small mosquitoes. They can sniff out aphid colonies, and then they lay their eggs next to them.

Within a few days, the larva will hatch and eat the aphids. The aphid predator midge can consume as many as fifteen aphids a day.

A Midge

Nematodes

These are natural parasites that are so small you can only see them with a microscope. They can kill approximately two hundred and fifty different types of larvae.

Familiarize yourself with the most common pests in your area. Then you will know how to deal with them.

Most common problems

It feels great to get your hydroponic system set up and established, especially as the crops start to appear. However, it is essential to maintain the environment and keep an eye out for some of the most common problems.

If you catch them fast enough, you will be able to react quickly and save the plant(s).

Common deficiencies in hydroponics:

- Calcium
- Magnesium
- Iron

Other problems include:

- Chlorosis - Yellowing of the leaves
- Necrosis - Death of the leaf

Nitrogen deficiency (N)

Yellow leaves can be a sign of a nitrogen deficiency. If nitrogen deficiency occurs, the plant will move the available nitrogen from the older leaves (bottom) to the new leaves (top). This means the bottom leaves will become yellow while the top leaves are still green. If you inspect the leaves carefully, you will see that the yellowing begins at the tip of the leaves, slowly making it's way to the center.

Phosphorus deficiency (P)

The leaves become darker, almost purple. The leaves will start to curl and will eventually drop. Phosphorus will be hard to spot at the beginning.

Potassium deficiency (K)

Potassium deficiency is also hard to spot. Older leaves (bottom) will form chlorosis (yellowing), and the edges of the leaf will turn brown with sometimes brown spots in the middle of the leaf.
The flowering of the plant is greatly diminished.
Calcium deficiency (Ca)
Calcium deficiency appears on new leaves. The edges of the leaf turn brown. Calcium deficiency is not to be confused with tip burn (too many nutrients) or lack of airflow.
It might be possible that your plants are developing signs of calcium deficiency even when there is enough calcium in the nutrient solution. This is because the environment you are growing in is too humid. The leaves cannot transpire water, which will lead to less nutrient uptake. One of these nutrients that fails to be taken up is calcium. Calcium is used to maintain cells. If calcium is not supplied, the new leaves will turn brown on the edges.
Decrease the humidity to fifty percent and install fans to circulate the air.

Magnesium deficiency (Mg)
Deficiencies can exist four weeks before you could see it happen. The leaves at the bottom will start to yellow between the veins (interveinal yellowing) with brown spots forming on the leaves. Over time, the leaves will almost completely turn white.
The older leaves will dry and curl up, eventually falling off the plant.

Iron deficiency (Fe)
Iron deficiency will lead to interveinal chlorosis at the new leaves (top). If you are using UV lights to remove algae from the water, you may have an iron deficiency. UV light makes iron precipitate out of the solution, making it unavailable for your plants to take up.

Too many nutrients
Too many nutrients can become a problem when you have nutrient build-up or just have added too many nutrients.
You should provide them with a quart or half of the dose of the mature plant.
Too many nutrients will result in nutrient burn, which are brown spots at the edge of the leaves. Not to be confused with calcium deficiency. The leaves will become dark green and start to curl up.
If your plants have nutrient burn, you need to flush them with a half-strength solution and lower the nutrient concentration.

Chapter 9

Tips and Tricks to Grow Healthy Herbs And Vegetables

Having a Plan

Making a plan and following it to the letter is an essential factor that can lead you to success in almost any field. The same is the case with hydroponic gardening.

You need to make a well-developed and well-made plan for your hydroponic garden to yield great results. This plan should include even the smallest of details. This will help you to keep a close eye on your plan and plants.

What exactly does making and having a plan entail? In simple words, having and making a plan entails having and noting down the nutritional needs of your plants, the light requirements of your plants and other essential details.

Basically, what you need to do is make a good catalog and note down every little detail of the plant that you want to cultivate. You should note down the feeding schedule, the nutrients, their strengths, the weaknesses of the nutrients and the changes in nutrient cycles, etc. Keeping all of this noted in a folder will help you not only in this crop cycle but will also help you in the subsequent crop cycles.

There are also ready-made plans available on the market. These plans are made according to the plants used. You can always buy such plans but remember to follow them properly. As hydroponic gardening is a delicate form of gardening, you may actually ruin your chances of a good produce if you do not follow your plan thoroughly. Thus, not only planning is essential but following the planned schedule is very important as well.

Nutrition

You should ideally note down these details. It is quite beneficial if you find out about the nutrients that you will need for a certain plant before you start growing it.

You should also find out about the dosage of the nutrients that you need to give to your plants weekly. This also includes the name of the nutrients that you are supposed to use.

Often a plant may need a certain nutrient at first and then may not need it at all as it matures. For instance, many plants require nitrogen in the beginning but when they are about to flower they need more phosphorus instead of nitrogen. This is true in the case of fruit bearing plants.

Ideally, you should consider spending a few bucks on an EC or TDS meter. These simple devices can help you to keep an eye on the strength of your solution. You can thus adjust the levels of your solutions accordingly to help your plants grow well.

Although it might be very tempting to try experimenting with home mixed plant food, if you are a beginner then you must avoid doing so, or else you can ruin your plants. Instead of doing this, you should buy professional hydroponic nutrient products that are easily available in the market. These systems are three-part systems and are very easy to use.

If you really want to try home mixed plant food, then you should do it when your plant system has grown and is thriving well.

Another thing that you must avoid is adding extra nutrient additives to your nutrient reservoirs. You may have seen people doing so, but these people are professionals or at least experienced. A beginner should not try experimenting with such things because it can ruin your system completely. When this happens, you can try experimenting with the nutrients by adding stuff like Silica, liquid seaweed, vitamin B1, etc. You can also try adding all of these together.

You also need to check your reservoir tank every day. Start with fresh water after every two weeks. It's the same in the case with nutrients. Have two reservoirs if possible one for nutrients and the other filled with plain water. The second reservoir technique will allow the water to become de-chlorinated and will also help it to come down to room temperature. This in turn will help you to protect your plant roots.

Root Health

In the last tip, we talked a little about root health. In this tip, let us look at the health of the roots in detail.

Roots are one of the most essential parts of a plant as they provide the plant with nutrients to survive and thrive. Consequently, if the roots suffer damage they simply cannot absorb nutrients. Roots serve as the base of the plant, so when the roots get damaged, the whole plant suffers. Bad roots cause rotting leaves and drying stem with low to zero yields. Thus, it is important to take care of the roots and keep them healthy.

You can do so by once again following the same old tip of keeping two reservoirs- one with the nutrients and an extra one with plain water for your next nutrient change. Another easy way to protect the roots is by limiting the amount of light that touches the nutrient solution. Light and moisture are two of most important things required for the growth of algae. Algae can ruin your roots and your plants as algae can invite and induce fungus, which can in turn invite gnats that can damage your plant's roots.

Lighting and Light Sources

Although a high yielding hydroponic garden can be easily constructed outdoors, most people who choose hydroponic gardening choose it because they want to construct an indoor garden. Outside, the light is provided by the best light source - the sun - but indoors you will need to make specific modifications to provide your garden with ample light.

There are no or very limited shortcuts when it comes to lighting a hydroponic garden. You need at least 40 watts bulb per square feet, but a 60-watt bulb is highly recommended. Even the kind and type of light is important. Ideally, metal halide light or a high-pressure sodium light will be the best option for your garden. A 600-watt or 1000 watt light is highly recommended.

In hydroponic gardening, lighting is one of the costliest, if not the costliest, system that you need to pay for. A good quality lighting system including the bulb, the reflector, and the ballast can cause you anything from $400 to $600.

Fluorescent lights are not of much use for healthy growth of plants. You should use these lights only for seedlings, clones or very young plants when they are still in their vegetative state. This is especially applicable to herbs, lettuce, spinach, etc.

Unfortunately, if you cannot simply find any other kind of lights and find yourself forced to use the fluorescent lights, then the only option you have is to use Tek or T5 lights. Although T5 lights do not produce as much heat as HID lights, they are effective. With the fluorescent lights, you also need to be careful about putting the tops of your plants too close to the bulb.

Maintaining the Temperature

Plants need to have ambient temperature conditions for best results. Even in hydroponic gardening, you need to maintain an ambient level of temperature. It is important to remember that the growth of the plants stops as soon as the temperature rises above 85 degrees unless obviously you are pumping in CO_2 continuously. Although HID lights are highly recommended lights for hydroponic gardening, you should not forget that these lights generate a lot of heat and thus temperature management can be a very painful task that you will have to do more frequently. You can reduce your workload by installing the ballast for your light outside your plant room. However, this will only help if you have the old school magnetic coil ballast, the digital one will not help you at all. The best option to regulate temperature is buying centrifugal or squirrel cage fans. These fans are helpful and useful in maintaining a good temperature level. You can also pump in air conditioning if you have access to it.

Manipulating Light

Some crops need a long daylight period while some need short daylight to induce flowering or fruiting. You need to study the behavior of your plants. You can also find information regarding the requirements of the individual plants online.
An important tip regarding lighting is you should always turn on and turn off the light source exactly at the same time every day. This will serve as a fake natural light system. To do these tasks with ease, consider buying a digital timer.
When the dark period is happening, do not interrupt it. Create a specially blacked out room for your gardening or, if it is not possible, then consider buying a blacked outgrow tent. Plants, especially young plants, are very sensitive to light and darkness thus an interrupted dark period can practically ruin your plants.

Choosing the Best Tools

A good worker should have good tools too. You simply should not start gardening unless and until you have all the equipment and tools needed for hydroponic gardening. You should ideally make a list of all the things that you might require. This may include a dark room, high-powered fan, a hydroponic gardening system, a light providing ambient light conditions, an oscillating fan, hydroponic nutrients, a TDS meter, or EC meter, if possible an air conditioner and a pH test kit. Consider spending some bucks on a digital timer and a thermometer as well.

Chapter 10

Starting Hydroponic Business

With the help of hydroponics, the entire image of a farmer has been altered, as it has helped farmers to cultivate even in sterile environments with the use of water. Hydroponic farming business is slowly gaining traction among the mainstream audience, with large business corporations and engineers starting to practice the same as well.

With the current market trends, it seems like herbs and small leafy green vegetables are a great way to start the business with. Mostly the NFT or Nutrient Film Technique is used for the process and the farmers have started to enjoy immense revenue and growth. In this article guide, we're going to discuss a step-by-step method about how you can start your own business related to hydroponics.

Understanding the Market in Your Locality

One of the most important hurdles that most businesses face in their starting phase is to know whether there is an existing market for the product you're planning to sell. In case you don't have a good market to sell, then you cannot make your business successful. You have to take your time in doing your research regarding where you're planning to sell and also to whom you're planning to sell. Try to not believe the words of any buyer or an agent. Any buyer will want more options in-front of him because more options mean more competitive pricing for a product. A buyer will always want oversupply of any product because then only the product can be obtained at a lower price point.

But you shouldn't delve too much into those insights and instead try to aim for a niche and as well as a desirable market - this is the combination that can earn you huge profits. It's always a better idea to enter a niche rather than a commodity market. For example, you can easily start a hydroponic business in rural areas because the options are far too little in the hands of the people living there.

It's believed that users who have a stable local market can be successful in this business. You can easily start with vegetables like lettuce, herbs, tomatoes, and even spinach. It will help you provide a good stable income. If you have a good local market, you can easily beat other growers in terms of yield, soil quality, and early harvest.

Learning About the Basics of the Business

If you're not wary about hydroponics farming, then you have to take lessons or classes in this specified subject. The first thing to do is have a deep understanding of how horticulture and agronomics take place. You have to read up on hydroponic farms to know if you're doing the business in the right manner. The main aim of hydroponics is to provide your customers with healthy as well as delicious fruits and vegetables. You can also work on other hydroponic farms for a short period so that you will come to know about the procedure in detail. Besides knowing about hydroponics, you also have to know about basic chemistry. For example, knowing about the composition of NaCl, NaOH, Calcium Nitrite, and the like.

Coming to the non-technical sector, you have to study and know about basic marketing principles. You also need to know about assembling the hydroponic systems like an engineer and learn about how to control your employees (if you're planning to hire). Apart from that, you have to lay importance on networking with other influential people in the same industry. This will aid you to get assistance and tips during emergencies. Finally, you also need to know a thing or two about book-keeping and accounting, so that you can at least kick-start the sales department in your business.

The Crop and the Type of Hydroponic System Technique
Once you've glossed over the previous two steps, it's time to decide on what crop you want to grow and therefore start your business. You have to select the crops, correlate them with the required climatic conditions and also know about the special equipment you need for the perfect growth.
The hydroponic irrigation technique will depend upon the crop you choose. For example, growing crops like cucumbers, tomatoes, eggplant, and peppers need a water culture technique (closed system) to grow in the best possible manner. On the other hand, growing lettuce or spinach can be done with drip irrigation (open system). Therefore, you can decide based on your preferences.

The Costs

The basic thing to start a new hydroponic business is to obtain a space for growing your crops. It should be kept in mind that most hydroponic farm businesses require a greenhouse. You can either build a greenhouse yourself or just rent it. You can build or rent a greenhouse depending upon your size preferences - it can be either big or small.
Besides space, you also need to invest in other materials and equipment as well. This includes crop seeds, nutrient solution, lighting, plumbing materials, UV filtration, systems for climate control, reservoirs for keeping the nutrient solution, etcetera. You also need to invest in a couple of desks and chairs, along with a desktop or laptop computer, a cash register and a fast broadband connection too. You have to set aside at least a couple thousand dollars for this kind of investment.
Knowing the Laws and Doing the Legal Formalities

Legal formalities include applying for the business' legal entity stature, opening up a current or business account, obtaining licenses, etcetera. You should make sure about the laws and regulations residing in your locality. Every rural, semi-urban and urban areas have their restrictions. You can easily consult with your local municipality commission, to know about the laws, the restrictions on the usage of water, all kinds of electrical requirements, use of chemical fertilizers, purchase, and use of hydroponic equipment, applying for insurance, etcetera.

Hydroponic farming is a new concept, so you should be prepared to educate people on the matter. You might have to educate employees of the city government and also that of your neighborhood too. Once you start obtaining your license and permits, it will also inspire other business people in the area to start their hydroponic businesses as well.

Investigating About the Suppliers

After you've done with your legal formalities, it's time to know about suppliers who are going to supply you with the required materials and equipment. These suppliers have been selling products for many years and therefore know a lot about the market demands and the crops that are most successful. You can proceed to take advice from them as well. The products that you obtain from your suppliers will ultimately decide the overall quality of your crops.

You have to get quotes from your suppliers before you make the investment. Use a spreadsheet to list all your costs regarding launching and also developing your business too.

Perform the Business Plan

Creating a business plan is very essential if you want your business to grow and have a long-term ambition.

A business plan contains all your business strengths, weaknesses, the aim of the business, etcetera. Further down the line, if you need investor's help in your business, this plan will help you get start-up funding.

After you've figured out all the above steps, it's time to do an analysis of your business as a whole. You have to examine its weaknesses, strengths, opportunities and also competitive threats too. You have to make a mission statement and then start writing your plan. In this plan, you have to describe your target customer, the revenue model, the marketing methods, backup plans, and other important information as well. You also have to create projections for your business revenue model. If you're new at this, you can obtain help from the administered office for small and medium-sized businesses.
Growing and Marketing the Business (or Brand)
A business starts to grow on the merit of its employees and therefore if you're planning to build a team, you have to do from the start. Adding employees in your business will help you focus on other important aspects of the business like revenue, business collaborations and investor funding. Employees will help in not only facilitating the plant growth but also monitoring it as well. Employees will also deliver the products to your customers, order any needed equipment or supplies, help in collecting the sale proceeds and also aid in maintaining the facility as well.

Moving on to the marketing side of things, if you're planning on selling your cultivated crops to most restaurants and supermarkets, then you need to invest more on the marketing aspect. This includes social marketing (Facebook and Instagram) and new media (YouTube). Only traditional marketing will not be sufficient. The most important thing that you should be doing here is to maintain your good relationships with the managers and owners of such a restaurant or supermarket chains.

You have to go the extra mile if you want to create more networking in the industry. You need to attend conferences related to food and also aim to build relationships with local businesses, who require fruits and vegetables - which you successfully grow in your hydroponic farm. This will help you build brand recognition.

Maintaining Quality

If you want customers to be loyal to your services and products, you have to provide them with good products at competitive prices. There should be a quality assurance team in your business that will help in maintaining the rigorous checks and thus maintain a benchmark or standard quality. Your product's quality should be better or even equal to your competitors. Besides, your business should be able to produce crops that are unique, which supermarkets and restaurants will not be able to obtain from other farmers or producers. You have to thrive in a very niche environment (or market) and you'll be raking in good profits from your business.

Charging the Customer and Making a Profit

There is a wide variety of prices that you can charge to your customers. But, you should keep the most important thing in mind - the price should be at least competitive. The price will depend on what you sell and grow. The pricing will also depend upon the market's demand and supply. If you have a unique product, then you can proceed to charge a little premium to your customers.

You can easily make a lot of money if you start big and your planning is right. In case you start small, then the profit might not be as big as you'd thought it to be. Once you start finding enough customers, then you can scale-up your business to meet the increased demands of the market. Also, you have to start selling to the customers directly, if you want the greatest return - there should be no middleman.

The Expenses of an Ongoing Business

Your agricultural farm built for hydroponic cultivation will require insurance, seeds, labor, equipment, delivery vehicles, facility, and etcetera. On top of that, you will also have employees working in your business as well, for which you have to provide the salary and bonuses. You should have significant capital to maintain your farm because you'll not only have to spend on new equipment to replace old ones, you also need to spend on utility expenses and hydroponic agricultural materials as well.

You should keep in mind that everything is related to long term commitment and should start with low risks. Firstly, start with a small investment and spend on those technologies that require less capital. After you've settled yourself and your brand name in the market along with a good percentage of returning customers, you can then think of expanding. Improve your services and products to create more credibility in the industry. Once you do that, your customer dependency will increase as a professional businessman.

Chapter 11

Basic Components of the System

Preparation of a hydroponic system is similar to purchasing a vehicle. You can purchase a sedan or a luxury model. The price and quality are up to you as the buyer. If you are traveling the economic route, this segment will guide you through the essential parts of your hydroponic system

Growing Chamber/Growing Tray

This space is where your roots grow and reach the nutrient systems to support the plants. The shape and size of the growing container will be determined by the type of plant or plants you will be growing. Choose materials for the chamber that will block the light to the roots. It will also protect the herbs, vegetables, and fruits from mold growth, pests, and high temperatures.

Grow Lights

You will need to choose a light specifically manufactured for hydroponically grown plants. Other lighting sources will not provide the correct light frequency for the plant to follow through with photosynthesis.

The Reservoir

The reservoir holds the nutrients that help your plants growth. Plastic is the best material to use because it can be cleaned easily. (Remember, it has to be opaque.) Exposure to direct lighting can cause damage to the plant roots. Wrap it with newsprint or paint it since this can also help prevent the growth of micro-organisms and algae in your nutrient solutions.

The Delivery System

The system can be as simple as PVC connectors and tubing – along with drip emitters and sprayers. If you choose any of the extras to your delivery system, be sure to keep them clean and have extra parts readily available if needed. The extras have a tendency to clog occasionally.

Pump

Hydroponics growing systems are available as an air pump or submersible pump unit:

- Air Pump: The air pump creates an air supply for the plant roots. If using the water culture system, the pump is optional. However, since the roots are submerged in the solution 24/7, it is still essential for the roots to receive via air supply. With other systems, the pumps will keep the reservoir oxygenated with the water and nutrients mixed well.

- Submersible Pump: The submersible pump is many times a fountain or pond pumping system. Just be sure to purchase the size which is adequate for your growing setup. Once again, be sure it is cleaned regularly. The pump can usually be found in standard gardening supply stores or hydroponics supply stores.

Temperature Control

Check what temperatures are ideal for your garden needs. Be sure not to place the system in an area prone to freezing that could cause damage to the plumbing as well as your precious plants.

The temperamental lettuce will die if the root mass temperature reaches 75°F. Be sure to keep a close watch on the temperatures during the sweltering heat of summer.

Timer

To encourage the growth of your plants, you will need a set schedule for sunlight. It will take one or two timers for your hydroponics kit. One control will provide the artificial lighting, and the other unit will control the on/off function for the pump (essential to aerate your roots).

Cords or Ropes for Smaller Systems

If ropes are used for systems housing large plants or more than two smaller ones, it should be at least ½-inches in diameter.

Nylon doesn't mold or rot, but cotton and other types of rope are effective. The length depends on the size of your hydroponic system.

Chapter 12
Tools You Will Need

As you venture into hydroponics farming, there are specific tools you need to get you started. Although there are several systems from which you shall choose, the kind of tools used in all of them is more or less the same.
The tools you will need include:

A Reservoir

From its name, the reservoir will be used for reserving the nutrient concentrate. The concentrate is typically a mixture of water and the required plant nutrients and depending on the kind of hydroponic system you choose to install; the liquid is pumped from it periodically into the growing chamber as set at the timers.

In some systems, the reservoir doubles as the growing chamber too, such that the plants grow suspending their roots in the nutrients concentrate 24 hours, every day.
You do not have to purchase a special reservoir; you can fashion it from almost any inert large container that you use to hold water, so long as it does not leak. The container should be able to hold enough of the solution to allow it to grow. In addition, the container should be opaque to prevent the rays of the sun from penetrating into the solution.
If the container available to you is not opaque, there are many ways to make it light proof. For example, you could wrap or cover it up with an opaque material, or you could paint over it. The idea behind the opaqueness is to prevent algae from growing on the inside of the container.

If the hustle of making your own reservoir seems a bit too much, you could also opt to purchase the commercial reservoirs, and they will serve you well.

A Growing Chamber

A growing chamber is one of the most critical parts of a hydroponic system because this is where the plant roots develop. The chamber is the container that holds the roots, provides support to the entire plant, and house the nutrient concentrate.

The chamber, just like the reservoir, should be kept from direct sunlight and extreme temperatures because these can introduce heat stress to the plants. In case of exposure to extreme temperatures, such as heat, the plants abort their fruits and flowers.

The size and shape of the growing chamber are dependent on the kind of hydroponic system you intend to run, and the plants you wish to grow. Plants that grow big roots will require a large growing chamber while those that develop small roots will be okay with just a small one. However, do not be stressed about sizes because any chamber size will make due so long as the plants you are growing get their deserved nutrients and space.

In your quest to find the best growing chamber, kindly keep off metallic containers because metals are subject to corrosion and they react with the nutrient concentrate. If you cannot purchase a commercial growing chamber, however, check around to see the non-metallic items you could transform into growing chambers. However, if you still need to maintain class and style while at it, you could opt for a commercial growing chamber; there are some fabulous makes available, and I am certain they will appeal to your pallet.

Delivery System

The delivery system is the system that delivers nutrients to the plant roots directly. The concept of this is quite simple, in fact, and can be customized to fit into any system you choose to take up and install. A typical delivery system must include connectors, PVC tubes, blue or black vinyl tubing, and tubing connectors, for garden irrigation.

Depending on the hydroponic system that you settle for, you can choose to use emitters and sprayers for the delivery system. Although the sprayers and emitters are quite useful, be prepared, however, for frequent clogs when the nutrients in the solution build up. Therefore, if you are looking forward to stress-free farming, avoid them as best as you can.

Submersible Pump

Most pumping systems have a submersible pump to regulate the pumping of the nutrient concentrate from the reservoir to the growing chamber. You can buy these pumps at home improvement stores or hydroponic shops in your area. The pumps come in varying sizes, and you just have to choose one that matches the size of your farm.

How do submersible pumps work, you ask? Well, the pumps are just impellers that take advantage of electromagnetic fields to spin then pump their water. It is easy to maintain them because the majority of the time, you are only required to clean the solution filter. If you bought your submersible pump without a filter, you could still make one by cutting some part of the furnace filter, ensuring that it fits the submersible pump. Besides the filter, you also need to clean the pump occasionally to ensure that there are no clogs that would obstruct the nutrients as they flow to the plants.

Air Pump

Although it is not compulsory that you make an air pump part of your hydroponic system, you ought to give it a thought because it comes with so many benefits. An air pump is also widely available in stores, and inexpensive, particularly if you are able to buy yours at a store that sells aquarium supplies. An air pump is primarily used to ensure that there is a steady supply of oxygen in the water so that the roots can absorb it for their respiration, in the growing chamber. The pump does this by pumping the air through the airlines, onto the air stones, which ten creates bubbles that bubble up into the nutrient solution.

In case you are using a water culture hydroponic system, for example, the air pump keeps the roots from drowning in the nutrient solution because they are kept suspended in it all day, every day. In other hydroponic systems, the air pumps are fitted into the reservoirs to keep pumping oxygen into the water, increasing the oxygen concentration in the water. Since the air pumps pump all day, they cause constant movement, which keeps the water and nutrients in it in constant motion. The circulation that results from the process ensures that the nutrients dissolve into the water evenly, at all times. The presence of oxygen in the water is also good because it prevents the growth of pathogens and microbes.

Timer

Not all hydroponics farmers need to time their operations with a timer, based on their choice of hydroponics system and its location. If your system is to be situated indoors, for example, and you have installed artificial lighting, you need to install a timer that will turn the lights off or on.

Drip and aeroponics systems also need a timer to control their submersible pump that controls the process of draining and flooding. It is important to take note of the fact that some types of aeroponics would need some special kind of timer to work properly.

Although the light and standard pump timers work very well, it is better to opt for a timer that has a 15 amperes rating other than 10 amperes rating because the former is often heavy duty and will have a cover that effectively protects it from water. You only have to check at the back of the packaging of the timer you choose to ensure that you have made a good choice.

But for those who may have a battery backup, a digital timer is not preferred over an analog one because once you unplug it from the power source, it loses all the data previously stored in it. Analog timers are a better choice for the additional benefit of having on and off settings. Therefore, as you go out to purchase a timer, ensure that yours has pins all around the dial, so that you get the analog kind, and avoid future regrets.

Growing Medium

The growing medium is essentially the substance on which the plants grow. It provides physical support to the plants, just like soil does, only that it is inert, not containing any minerals or living organisms. Different systems demand different growing mediums. For example, while other systems use peat moss, Rockwool or lava stone as the growing medium, aeroponics system uses air as the growing medium.

Nevertheless, the right kind of medium is one that retains moisture in such a way that the water solution will not need to be pumped in continually, every single minute.

Growing Lights

Grow lights: you can have them you can stay without them. They are an optional part of the system because it all depends on where you intend to plant your garden. You may end up using natural light or having to take up artificial lighting for your plants. If possible, opt for natural lighting because it is free, and will not add to the cost of setup as you purchase the new equipment and its accompanying maintenance costs.

If, however, you cannot find any good lighting at the place you intend to plant your garden by having lots of exposure through the window or having a sunroom, or that the time of the year does not allow enough lighting through, you may need to include some supplemental artificial lighting in your set up budget.

Kindly realize that your ordinary bulbs cannot be used as grow lights: grow lights are specially made light bulbs that emit light containing special color spectrums that mimic natural light. Your plants will take in these color spectrums and use them to carry on the process of photosynthesis, hence the leaf growth, flower formation, and fruit growth. Realize also that the intensity and type of light that the plant has access to, by large, determines its photosynthetic abilities.

Most hydroponic kit systems will come with complimentary light fixtures, but if you are setting up a DIY (Do It Yourself) garden, piecing together the equipment you need, you will need to purchase lighting fixtures.
The most effective lighting for a hydroponics system is the High-Intensity Discharge (HID) light fixture made up of either Metal Halide (MH) bulbs or High-Pressure Sodium (HPS) bulbs. The HPS, in particular, emits a red or orange-looking light, which works well for plants, particularly in their vegetative growth stage.

Another type of lighting used is T5. It produces fluorescent light of a high output, and this lighting consumes low energy and only a little heat. The T5 is suitable for when growing plant cuttings, and for growing plants with short growth cycles. Ensure that the light is kept on a time so that the lighting will go on and off at the same time, each day.

PH Testing Kit

If you don't test the pH of your nutrient solution from time to time, you will be running your farm purely by guesswork, subjecting your entire investment to a trial-and-error game. The reality is that for your plants to thrive in the hydroponic garden you have set up, there needs to be a balanced pH, and using a pH testing kit, you can regularly check on your garden to determine whether the pH of the nutrient solution is optimal. If the pH is too low, you can adjust by bringing it up, and if it's too high, you can lower it also.

On a related note, besides the pH meter, you will also need equipment to measure the temperature and the PPM of the water. You could also purchase the equipment you would need to measure the humidity and temperature of the grow room. If, for example, you find that you need to adjust the humidity in the room, use a dehumidifier or a humidifier, to ensure that the plants do not dry out and that they do not dampen.

A fan or any other equipment that can be used to improve the air circulation in the room would also be welcome. Although a small oscillating fan may work for a beginner, you will need a more sophisticated fan as your garden grows, one with an intake and an exhaust system.

The Nutrient Solution

While the nutrient solution is not a tool, you will need to set it aside as you set your tools aside, in readiness for the setup of your garden. As we have established many times so far, the nutrient solution will be the primary source of nutrients for your plants for them to thrive.

The nutrient solution provides three primary macronutrients that can be found in most fertilizers: potassium, phosphorus and nitrogen, and a host of 10 other micronutrients that may not be found in the fertilizers, yet the plants need them to survive, grow and reproduce. Some of these micronutrients include zinc, molybdenum, boron, copper, iron, chloride and manganese.

As a beginner, it may benefit you to purchase an already mixed solution offering a balance of all the nutrients indicated, but as you gain more experience, you will find it easier to mix create your own nutrient solution, one that will provide the plants with all the nutrients they require.

The fertilizers or nutrients used in the hydroponic system you can find in both dry and liquid forms, and there are both organic and synthetic kinds. Either type you choose will be dissolved in water to come up with the nutrient solution that we have associated with the hydroponic system severely. As you look around the store, you will find that there are some specific fertilizers or nutrients specifically designed for hydroponic farming, and if you use them, you are bound to receive good results, provided you follow all instructions indicated on the packaging. Kindly avoid using standard soil fertilizers in a hydroponic system because their mixing formulas are specifically designed for garden soil, not for direct infusion into the roots as it happens in hydroponics. While still on the point of hydroponic fertilizers, ensure that you choose the kind of hydroponic nutrient that is designed for your particular needs. For example, you will find that some fertilizers are designed for flowering plants, while others are good for promoting vegetative growth such as that used for lettuce. If you apply the latter to a flowering plant, you will promote the growth of the leaves rather than the formation, enlargement, and blossoming of flowers.

The Quality of the Water Used

The solubility of water and its ability to deliver the nutrients you dissolved into it is affected both by the salt level of the water, as can be seen from the PPM, and the water pH. Typically, hard water has a high mineral content, and this fact keeps it from dissolving the minerals as effectively as the water that has a low mineral content. Therefore, in the event that the water you have for your project is hard, you will need to filter it out to take out the high mineral content.
The ideal water pH for making the nutrient solution is between 5.8 and 6.2, which is somewhat acidic. If your water is not at this pH level, you can use some chemicals to adjust it so that the pH gets within this ideal range.

The Conditions of the Room

It is of utmost importance, and great value, that the hydroponic system be set in the right conditions. Some of the elements you ought to check to ensure that the conditions are right include the carbon dioxide levels, relative humidity, temperature, and air circulation.

The humidity level is ideal if it ranges between 40% to 60% relative humidity. If the humidity gets to higher levels, it may lead to the formation of powdery mildew and other kinds of fungi.

The ideal temperature should range from 68 to 70F. If the temperatures are higher, the plants will become stunted, and if it gets even higher, the roots may start to rot.
The level of carbon dioxide, CO_2, is of most importance in the grow room. The best way to ensure that there is an adequate supply of it is by ensuring that the room has a free flow of air. As your farm or garden becomes bigger, you could now begin to supplement the CO_2 levels in the room because the more the gas is available in the growth room, the faster the growth of crops.

A Greenhouse

Any serious hydroponics gardener should aim for the ultimate gardening tool, a greenhouse. A greenhouse offers a farmer lots of advantages including complete climatic control, a lot of growing room, and access to natural lighting. If you are serious about increasing the output from your hydroponics garden, then the greenhouse is the way to go. It may seem like an ambitious project at first, but the return is that you get to have a larger supply of nutritious, safe and high-quality food for your nutrition, and to supply to other people, in exchange for money.

Chapter 13

Hydroponic Systems Equipment

You now have the basics figured out; now it is time to discover how to install your chosen hydroponic unit and begin your garden. You can purchase a system from a gardening supply store or hydroponic supply store, but if you are handy, it is fun to build your own.

By now, you have decided whether you want it in your home, on the porch, or any other location that is suitable for your chosen products. Just so you have an idea of how you can start from scratch, the wick system is the simplest as shown. Several setups are shown with the list of parts needed to provide you with some insight on how involved preparing your system can be if you choose to take the do-it-yourself route. The choice is yours, whether you purchase a ready-to-install unit or go the piece-by-piece method; Let's get started!

The Wicking Method

List of Parts

- Container for the reservoir
- Container for the plant
- Substrate
- Material Strips – ex. good wicking rope or felt

How to Assemble

The easiest of the hydroponics systems to install is wicking. All you need is a hole in the lid of a container as your reservoir. Add 2 wick strips and pull that through the plant container. Add substrate and the plant.

Ebb & Flow System

You can add as many systems as you wish but this one is for six plants:

List of Parts

- 6 (2-liter empty bottles) Cleaned and sterilized
- 8 (¾-inch) PVC - T-connectors
- ¾-inch PVC tubing
- 1 ¾-inch x ½-inch reducing connector (for connecting to the barbed connector)
- ½-inch barbed & threaded PVC connector (for connecting tubing to the PVC)
- 6 (¾-inch) PVC straight coupling connectors (for attaching the bottles to PVC tubing
- 7 (¾-inch) PVC elbow connectors
- PVC glue
- Epoxy or hot glue gun
- Water pump
- 10-20-gallon storage tote
- Black and white spray paint
- ½-inch black vinyl tubing
- Optional: Air lines, stones, & aquarium air pump

How to Assemble

Remove the bottle bottoms and punch drain holes in them using a drill or hot metal poker. Flip the bottle upside down and slide the prepared bottom back into the bottle.
Grind off several threads from the bottleneck so the ¾-inch wide PVC tubing connector will fit properly. You may have to use some epoxy or a hot glue gun to keep them in position. Once the glue dries, cover the opening of the PVC connector (very important), so paint doesn't get into the connector.
Paint the bottleneck with black paint. When dry, apply a few coats of white paint.

Build the Base: Use a hacksaw to cut the tubing, a tape measure to cut all pieces equally, and a sharp knife blade to remove the burs.

The spacing you use will depend on which plants you grow. Pay close attention to the short segments of ¾-inch tubing which will be point straight up from the T-connections where bottles will be placed; (2-3 in. is good).

Once the base is set, place the bottles on it. The bottles go on first, so you will know what height you will have to construct the overflow tube.

Do not glue the bottles because you will need to move them later for maintenance. Once the bottle is set, work on the overflow side. The water level of the bottles should be about 2 inches below the substrate placed in the bottles.

When done with connecting the tubes, glue all of the PVC connections. (Omit the ones where the bottles are connected to the rest of the hydroponic system.) To prevent air pocket damage, drill a small hole in the top of the overflow tube.

Set up the Reservoir: The easiest way is to build the reservoir is to place it right under the overflow tube. Line it up and make a small hole where the tube fits. Repeat the procedure as you did with the bottles; first with black and then with white paint layers.

Deep Water Culture System

List of Parts

- Air pump (30-60-gallon aquarium or larger)
- Storage tote
- Air stones
- Air line
- Substrate
- 8 (3-inch) net baskets for growing chambers
- White and black spray paint

How to Assemble

Prepare the storage crate/tote by cutting 8 holes in the tote (evenly spaced). You will be using a 3-inch net basket, so you will need to take precise measurements, or the container will fall through.

Spray the top of the lid and the bottom outside of the crate with black paint to prevent constant exposure of the root system to sunlight.

Once the black is dry, spray several layers of white. The white will help reflect some of the harmful rays and help regulate the temperatures. (Water temperature should never be higher than 80°F.)

Cut another – smaller – hole in the center of the lid (wide enough for the flexible air hose to go through).
Arrange the air stones in the grow chamber/storage tote. Connect the air lines to the tote and run the lines the hole in the lid. Next, just close the lid and connect the lines to the air pump. (Arrange the air pump 6-8 inches above the water line in the tote to prevent water from reaching the pump.)
Make sure the tote is level and place the baskets on the lid.
Fill the unit with the nutrient solution, keeping in mind that the baskets will hang approximately ½ -inch in the water.
Arrange the substrates into the net pots and add your plants.
Expand anytime you want to increase your crops.
Whether you choose to use hydroponics equipment purchased from a dealer or choose to make it a hobby, you will be sustaining your food supply.

Aeroponics

List of Parts

- 1 ½-inch x 12-inch cut-off threaded poly riser
- 1 (5-gallon) bucket with lid
- 1 (360°) ½-inch plastic head threaded sprinkler head
- 1 (317-gallon per hour) ½-inch threaded pump
- 1 timer (for 30-minute increments)
- (Desired amount) Net pots with rubber foam lids
- Saw to cut the poly riser
- 1 Hole saw
- Drill for the hole saw
- Sharpie
- Safety glasses

How to Assemble

Determine how many pots you want for your system.
Paint the outside of the bucket and lid with a layer of black. When dried, follow up with two layers of white. Let it dry fully before using.

Cut the holes for the net pots using careful precision using a saw or drill.
Screw the threaded poly cut-off riser to the pump after cutting the riser to the preferred height. Add it to the sprinkler head. Add the riser with the pump and the sprinkler head. Place in the bucket.
Run the pump through the net pole and plug into the timer. Set it for 30 minutes off and 30 minutes on.
Arrange the substrate in the pots and add your plants.

Chapter 14

Choosing the Best Lighting Medium For Your Hydroponic Plants

To upgrade the development of your plants, you have to have the privilege develop lights. It is critical to make reference to know that despite the fact that glaring lights can be utilized to enhance characteristic light, they can't, all alone, give the range of light required by plants.
Metal Halide and High-Pressure Sodium Lights were created to discharge a range of light that impersonates the nature of light radiating from the sun. Metal Halide lights are the nearest you can get to daylight. They produce progressively a higher extent of blue light that is incredible for supporting vegetative development.

High weight sodium lights then again produce light that spreads a greater amount of the red-orange range. They last more, consume more splendid and expend a lower measure of vitality than their metal halide partners, despite the fact that they produce a smaller range of light.

For the best outcomes, it is suggested that you join the utilization of the two kinds of lights to give light that is as close as conceivable to the full range of daylight. Moreover, you can utilize light reflectors and movers to cover a more extensive space with less lights.

Fake lighting techniques
What Are Grow Lights?

In its least difficult definition, a develop light is a counterfeit wellspring of light, ordinarily an electric light, which is intended to invigorate the development of plants by radiating an electromagnetic range ideal for photosynthesis. Such lights are regularly utilized in applications where there is an absence of characteristic light or extra light is required. State for instance, throughout the winter months, develop lights can be utilized to supply extra long stretches of light for plant development. It develops vegetables and natural products develop inside too.

In enormous scale, indoor cultivating tasks, develop lights can totally supplant direct daylight. Notwithstanding, develop lights don't generally need to imitate daylight precisely. In numerous applications, they can outflank daylight.

Sorts of Grow Lights

There are three essential sorts of develop lights accessible for indoor urban cultivating: Fluorescent develop lights, HPS or HID develop lights, and LED develop lights.

1. Fluorescent Grow Lights. Fluorescent develop lights are utilized for developing herbs and vegetables inside. They are two sorts, including fluorescent cylinders and Compact Fluorescent Lights (CFLs). Fluorescent cylinders come in a wide range of forces. They last more and are more vitality productive than glowing bulbs- - the normal bulbs that have been lighting homes for quite a long time. Bright light bulbs are flimsy and can without much of a stretch fit into little spaces. With respect to drawbacks, they require a weight to direct present and the cylinders require a stand, instead of a traditional attachment.

Such necessities can add to the expense of establishment.

Then again, CFLs have turned out to be progressively basic in family use and not simply in indoor urban cultivating. CFLs utilize just 20 to 30% of the vitality devoured by customary brilliant bulbs and their life expectancy is six to multiple times longer. They are by a long shot the least expensive among every one of the three significant sorts of develop lights. One outstanding favorable position with CFL bulbs is they don't emanate abundance heat, enabling ranchers to keep the lights nearer to the plants. This low warmth highlight makes it very vitality effective too.

2. HPS Grow Lights: High-Pressure Sodium (HPS) lights have developed in prominence and are surpassing fluorescent cylinders and bulbs. These lights are progressively normal among business and experienced indoor cultivators and the innovation behind them is settled, effectively more than 75 years of age.
The issue with HPS is that it delivers a lot of warmth. All things considered, you should keep the lights a decent good ways from the plants. They require a lot of venture to set up and keep up. Subsequently, HPS isn't suggested for little producers.

3. Driven Grow Lights: While the beginnings of LED innovation initially rose in the mid 1900s, the red and blue LEDs ideal for indoor cultivating started being utilized only preceding the 2000s.

Driven develop lights are the most vitality proficient among each of the three essential kinds of develop lights. These sources can be put more distant from plants while as yet delivering enough light without expending a lot of vitality. CFLs are practically half less proficient than LED develop lights. The warmth generation by LED develop lights is almost zero. Above all, LED performs best to make an ideal indoor condition to make practically any sort of nourishment.

The expense of LED lights is higher than other two sorts, be that as it may. Also, laborers working in indoor ranches need to utilize eye insurance as LEDs can be unsafe to human eyes.

Characteristics of lighting techniques

The most straightforward approach to arrangement fake lighting for an indoor nursery is to recollect these dependable guidelines. 40 watts for each square foot for high light plants like tomatoes and peppers and 25 watts for every square foot for low light plants like lettuce and verdant plants.
This implies for an average 4' x 4' space, you would require 400 watts of lighting to develop low light adoring plants, and 600 watts of lighting to develop high return plants like huge tomato and pepper plants.

Joining Natural And Artificial Lighting Techniques

When thought about two unmistakable ways of thinking in agriculture, the line among indoor and open air development is being obscured. Profoundly complex, all year nurseries are at the front line of this combination development as they use the accepted procedures of the two strategies in an innovative give and take. These tasks use the sun's vitality to control basic plant capacities while actualizing indoor developing advancements like light sensors, power outage covering frameworks, dehumidifiers, and mechanical radiators to mirror indoor ecological controls in open air settings.

Supplemental Lighting

Maybe the most essential innovative application in these current nurseries is that of supplemental lighting.

In indoor planting, lighting is one of the most significant elements directing the result of a gather. Be that as it may, it is additionally perhaps the costliest component of an activity, with an overhead of in any event $400 per unit for 1,000W twofold finished high weight sodium (HPS) lights and $800 per unit for similar light emanating diodes (LEDs). Taken to a business scale, this overhead can demonstrate very scary as it is exclusively dependent upon these counterfeit light sources to nourish each square inch of a gigantic nursery overhang. At that point there is the galactic expense of running the lights in these huge scale set-ups. Some 10,000-square-foot distribution center develops have detailed power bills as much as $12,000 month to month.

Nonetheless, current nurseries utilize best practices from both indoor and outside development. With regards to lighting, this implies utilizing a cautious parity of daylight and supplemental light. It's changing the manner by which individuals develop crops outside.

SUREFIRE TECHNIQUES TO HELP YOU MAINTAIN YOUR HYDROPONICS SYSTEM TO PREVENT PLANT DISEASES AND KEEP PESTS UNDER CONTROL

Here are a few hints on the best way to capitalize on your new develop room.

#1. Picking the Perfect Measure of Room For Your Plants
The main thing to remember before you set up your develop room: the amount you will develop. When you have a smart thought of what number of plants will consume the indoor develop room, you can decide how a lot of room you have to leave between the plants and the light source you will require.
#2. Finding The Correct Gear
Utilizing the correct gear in your develop room configuration can positively be the contrast among progress and disappointment.

Utilizing the right LED lights will help since the innovation in them is at long last making up for lost time to the lights most expert cultivators have utilized for quite a long time. Likewise make certain to have a period change to consequently kill the lights on and for when your plants explicitly need it.

Your cannabis develop room can't flourish without ventilation. With no moving air, the plants will overheat and kick the bucket. It is ideal to utilize a wind stream framework and a fan for predictable air course so the temperature and carbon dioxide will spread equitably all through the room.

At long last, a waterproof floor is significant in your develop room arrangement and configuration just as an approach to check the stickiness. Having the appropriate measure of dampness noticeable all around will help the development of your plants, and yet guarantee there isn't an excessive amount of stickiness, which will avoid organism and form development. In the event that you need to go down the hydroponic way, it will diminish the requirement for pesticides and herbicides. Likewise, hydroponically developed plants become quicker and can lessen water utilization by up to 90% rather than ordinary agrarian strategies.

#3. Give Appropriate Supplements to Your Plants

When planning a develop room, make certain to utilize living or natural soil in your pots. As indicated by Cannabis and Tech Today, "Living soil is wealthy in microorganisms and microfauna, which separate supplements in the dirt and make them simpler for the plant to retain. Natural soils and supplements are not just economical, plants developed with these strategies will in general have more strong taste and flavor profiles than buds developed utilizing non-natural techniques."

Simply recollect that it will be critical to give nitrogen, potassium, and phosphorus for your plants, however don't try too hard. Nitrogen lethality is excessively regular of a ruin for producers.

#4. Guarantee Your Plants are Sheltered and Secure

It ought to abandon saying that you won't be a fruitful cannabis rancher if your plants are devastated or demolished. When you investigate your develop room arrangement and configuration, are there enough bolts for the entryways? Are there in any case somebody could vandalize the area? It may likewise be ideal to think about putting resources into cameras. It is an additional expense, yet it could wind up sparing you a great deal of cash contrasted with having your plants taken or devastated.

Those are only a couple of proposals on the best way to capitalize on your cannabis develop room. Make certain to take a gander at all the various choices you have and choose what is the best way for you to guarantee the most beneficial and most strong yields conceivable.

Extra Equipment

Notwithstanding the fundamental hydroponic arrangement, it's a smart thought for learners to put resources into a couple of extra things.

You will need meters to test the PPM and pH of the water, just as the temperature and relative stickiness of the room. There are some mix meters accessible that will test the pH, PPM, and water temperature. You can likewise buy meters that measure the temperature and additionally the mugginess in your develop room.

Contingent upon your atmosphere, you may require a humidifier or dehumidifier to change the relative dampness in the develop space to an ideal level.

You might need to have some sort of fan or air course gear to improve the wind current in your develop room. Indeed, even a basic swaying fan functions admirably, yet as you get increasingly experienced, you might need to put resources into a progressively refined admission and-fumes framework.

Great Starter Plants

A few plants that work very well for apprentices simply learning the essentials of hydroponic cultivating include:

Greens, for example, lettuce, spinach, Swiss chard, and kale
Herbs, for example, basil, parsley, oregano, cilantro and mint
Tomatoes
Strawberries
Hot Peppers

Frameworks For More Advanced Gardeners

Two progressively confused frameworks are best saved for hydroponic nursery workers who have just taken in the nuts and bolts: the N.F.T. framework, and the aeroponic framework.

N.F.T. represents Nutrient Film Technique. It utilizes a steady progression of water/supplement arrangement that streams always in a circle from a repository through a developing plate, where plant roots are suspended in air and ingest supplements as the arrangement streams by. Be that as it may, if something turns out badly with the siphon system, the roots can dry immediately when the stream stops. This framework requires a client who can screen the apparatus and fix it rapidly if issues emerge.

An aeroponic framework is a cutting edge technique where plant roots are suspended in air and are clouded at regular intervals with a water/supplement arrangement. It is a profoundly powerful strategy yet one that requires complex siphons and sirs. In the event that the hardware has issues, the plant finds on will dry and pass on rapidly.

Hydroponic Gardens Require Certain Plant Nourishment

1 – Using the Wrong Plant Food

It very well may entice to purchase a sack of compost from your neighborhood nursery place for use in your hydroponic framework. All things considered, it's tied in with conveying supplements, isn't that so?

Not really! Customary manure may not weaken totally through your framework. Moreover, it can stop up channels and cylinders. Rather, put resources into compost intended for hydroponic frameworks. Hydroponic compost, which is accessible as fluids or granules, meets the developing prerequisites you need in a dirt less or soil-light nursery by giving extra supplements your plants may some way or another miss.

Poor sanitation can prompt develop room vermin and plant illnesses

2 – Not Focusing on Sanitation

Try not to give your hydroponic nursery zone a chance to turn into a trash canister. Your sanitation propensities can majorly affect the strength of your plants and your whole hydroponic framework.

Some fundamental cleaning needs that you should address:

· Keeping floors perfect and dry
· Sanitizing and cleaning framework gear
· Sanitizing and cleaning apparatuses
· Sanitizing and cleaning compartments
· Discarding plant squander
· Without appropriate sanitation, you can spread plant ailment or give nuisances concealing spots and sustenance.

3 – Opting Not to Learn

Present day hydroponic frameworks have been around since the mid twentieth century, and in that time a great deal of data and direction has been made accessible. School courses are instructed on it. Several books are accessible. You can even discover a ton hydroponic developing data here on the

To put it plainly, don't go only it! Peruse up and make an arrangement for your hydroponic nursery. Converse with other hydroponic nursery workers and offer thoughts. The more you know before setting up your nursery, the happier you'll be when you're prepared to gather.

4 – Over-watering

A typical issue individuals have when developing plants in a hydroponic framework is overwatering. Overwatering plants can hinder their development and decay the root frameworks. In case you're attempting to think about your plants, it's enticing to water them constantly, however you should adhering to the plant's watering guidelines.

Chapter 15

The World of Hydroponics

You will experience many advantages by using hydroponics including water and space savings, bigger yields, and many others. You can choose which system will best work with your designated spaces by planning ahead of the time you want to begin your crops.

Hydro Plant Growing Advantages

Bigger Yields: You will discover that using our hydroponic system will yield larger more frequent harvests.
No Soil: Your system blesses you with no more soil-based chores. The hoes, tilling, plowing, manure, and wheelbarrows are gone!

Water Saving: Plants are given only as much water as they need. With traditional watering, much of the water is evaporating, and your plants are not receiving that water. According to the experts, your water consumption for gardening will be reduced by 70-80%.

Space Saving: The system is so compact that you will need very little space for your growing needs. The root system doesn't spread out like it would if embedded in a soil bed. Plants are grown close together thus saving your living space.
Fewer Weeds, Pests, and Diseases: Hydroponic systems eliminate the soil that can collect foreign materials, making these problems almost disappear.

Prevents Fertilizer Overuse: The hydroponic environment is directly controlled leading to minimal waste. Animals and humans benefit from the cleaner and non-contaminated water supplies.

Faster Growth Versus Traditional Methods: The plant will no longer need to 'hunt' for its water supply, which in turn provides an efficient growing system and quicker yields. You achieve a lot more results with a lot less labor!

Planning the Garden

You have to focus on where to set up your hydroponic system. The correct location will depend on your space which is dictated by how many plants you want to grow in your gardening area.

First, consider the agricultural zone in which you live, zone one through twelve. You will need to study which plants grow best in your zone belt. For example, hemlock plants are considered a zone six or seven because they grow in colder areas whereas tropical plants are in zone nine through twelve. Make certain when you arrange your garden that you have plants that will be compatible with the same temperature and humidity factors. Each of these elements will be crucial factors in the plant's growth.

Space and Design of the System

Many things need to be considered when it comes to details in the chosen system. First, you will need to determine which plants have the largest root system and how many plants can share a container. You also have to decide which plants will take over or kill other plants.
The best method is to consider using just one tray, bucket, or planter for each plant. With the design in mind, you have a clearer idea of how to arrange the plants to make the best use of your space.

Some plants will vine which essentially means they will spread to the sides or grow taller. Some examples of vining plants include tomatoes, cucumbers, and strawberries. You can keep some of the plants under control by pruning away non-essential leaves and stems – remembering you need to leave enough foliage to protect the fruit from the sun if you are gardening outside.

Designing your space will allow you to take advantage of empty spaces such as a planter along a window of 6-inches x 4 feet. Use your corners and other areas in your home more efficiently - if you decide you want to garden inside. You can use the same principals outside if your space is also limited in that area.

Types of Hydroponic Systems

As you see from the diagrams below of several of the systems, they are not difficult to assemble and make functional. Your choice will depend on how much space you have and what you want to grow. This segment should provide you with enough insight to decide which one will be established in your home.

The Wick System

The Hydroponic Wick System provides the simplest setup for hydroponic gardening (Image 1). The nutrients are stored in the reservoir with the wick drawing the nutrients when the plant roots require them. Use some cotton or similar material and encircle the growing medium with one end of the cotton/wick dropped into the nutrient solution. In turn, it is absorbed to plant's root system.

You can simplify the process by discarding material and using a medium that can absorb the nutrients as needed. Vermiculite or perlite is an ideal choice. You should avoid mediums including peat moss, coconut coir, or rock wool with this system. The use of those mediums can cause too much of the nutrient solution in the plant, resulting in suffocation of the plant.

Deep Water Culture (DWC)

The DWC technique, also known as the reservoir method (Image 2) is uncomplicated and is superb for a beginner. It is easily maintained in a container garden. The most difficult skill required is monitoring the static solution. You will utilize a pump to keep the plant's oxygen levels adequate. The growing chamber and reservoir are basically the same part. The roots are submerged completely in the nutrient solution with an air pump that prevents the roots from drowning.

The Drip System

As you see, the drip system (Image 3) functions with the use of a timer control accompanied with a submerged pump. When activated, the timer will drip the nutrient solution to the base of each plant using a small drip line. The excess runs off and is recycled. As a result, you have much less maintenance. There will be no need to monitor the pH level in the reservoir! The professionals suggest using peat moss, coco coir, or rock wool.

Note: You can also choose to use a 'faster-draining' medium, but you will also need to use a 'faster-dripping' emitter. The emitters/drippers are notorious for clogging. (If you are using organic nutrients, you will more than likely have this type of issue.)

Ebb-Flow (Flood & Drain)

A great starting point for beginners is this uncomplicated system which is readily purchased as a kit or it can also be engineered by you in your home. The submersible pump circulates the nutrient solution between the grow tray and the reservoir. The excess flows back down into the reservoir, making nutrient solution efficiency top-grade.

For plants that are accustomed to having times of dryness, the ebb and flow will be a good choice. Some plants will flourish during those times since the root system will grow larger seeking moisture. As it grows, it absorbs more of the nutrients.

Aeroponics

The full name is Aero-garden Aeroponics System. The drip sprayer is set up using a timer to mist the plants with nutrient solution. The roots only uptake the required nutrients which increases the system's efficiency. Leftovers are recycled into the reservoir. You must maintain the root hydration with the surrounding humidity levels to sustain its growth. This technique is much faster in comparison to plants grown in soil.

Nutrient Film Technique (NFT)

The NFT method (Image 6) is used in most areas by commercial growers and requires frequent monitoring and a more complicated system. It requires a pump, reservoir, and a growing tray – all placed on a tilt which is a bit more complicated than the other units described. This unit is excellent for growing lettuce or other short-term crops but not ideal for indoor growing.

Contemplations

You will need to consider which unit is right for you. These are a few items you must consider in the process:

- What type of plants will you be growing? (For example – veggies, fruits or herbs.)
- Consider the size of the root and the amount of oxygen necessary for the root system.
- How large with the plant be as a grown plant?
- What types of plants and how many times you want to replant?
- How difficult is the system chosen to repair or maintain?
- Is the assembly and breakdown of the system simple or difficult?

Hydroponics Versus Soil Gardening – The Final Stand
You need to recall the advantages of using soil before you make your final plunge into hydroponics. Consider these differences using soil versus hydroponics:

Soil Doesn't Use Electricity: Light sources and electricity are used in some of the hydroponic systems to aerate the roots with the use of bubbles.

Initial Cost: Setups are more expensive versus just using soil. However, you also consider the unnecessary pesticides, fertilizer, and extra amounts of water you need using soil.
Less Bacterial and Mold Growth: This is perhaps the most daunting of the disadvantages. The moist environment required using hydroponics can cause mold growth and possible bacteria if the plants are not properly maintained. Now that you better understand the types of systems and some of the possible 'quirks,' it's time to see how the system functions in your home.

CPSIA information can be obtained
at www.ICGtesting.com
Printed in the USA
BVHW091939180521
607636BV00009B/1029